Some Run With Feet of Clay

Some Run With Feet of Clay

Jeannette Clift

Fleming H. Revell Company
Old Tappan, New Jersey

Unless otherwise identified, Scripture quotations are from the King
James Version of the Bible.

Scripture quotations identified PHILLIPS are from THE NEW TESTA-
MENT IN MODERN ENGLISH (Revised Edition), translated by J. B.
Phillips. © J. B. Phillips 1958, 1960, 1972. Used by permission of Macmil-
lan Publishing Co., Inc.

Library of Congress Cataloging in Publication Data

Clift, Jeannette.
    Some run with feet of clay.

    1. Clift, Jeannette. 2. Christian biography—
Texas—Houston. 3. Actors—Texas—Houston—Biog-
raphy. 4. Houston, Texas—Biography. 5. Chris-
tian life—1960-   I. Title.
BR1725.C524A37   248'.4   77-20907
ISBN 0-8007-0901-2

TO my husband,
Lorraine George

Contents

Introduction

There are few things more terrifying to me than place cards. Little sketched creatures or flowers of bright embroidery do nothing to dispel the horror that engulfs me as I circle the table. *Where is my name?*

Did my gracious hostess lose thought of me in the computing of her guest list? Did my long-lost invitation specify another time and another place? *Where is my name?*

I look quickly at the pack circling the table with me like Indians attacking settlers. Each face looks welcomed, assured, and loved. They point out their names with sophisticated glee. I detect a certain smugness as they watch me continuing the circuit. *They* are wondering how I got *in*—I am wondering how I get *out*. Could I grab a tray and apron and pass myself off as one of the service staff? *Where is my name?*

Suddenly, a flicker of hope similar to that of Florence Nightingale's candle flashes through the maze of greenery. There! Held aloft by a broken china jonquil is my own name. I was invited. I was expected. I have a place, and will be fed.

In much the same way, I circled a more significant table, a table provided for the banquet of life. I looked for a token of personal welcome and found none. Those around me found assurance in ways that had no meaning to me.

9

In kindness they turned to share their assurance with me. Books and pamphlets were showered upon me, like ticker tape upon a Wall Street parade. They only added to my confusion.

I was introduced to heroic leaders, and found myself intimidated by their courage and excluded by their example. I decided my only way out was to fake it, and strongly suspected that some of them had made the same choice. I tried with all the artistry I knew, and only felt anger and frustration.

Instead of reverence, I sensed an appetite within me for attacking the joy of those who sat with me. I wanted to tear into their holiness and prove it to be as hollow as mine. I resented being left out of all the finger-licking eating that went on so noisily around me.

I knew why I was excluded. I didn't measure up to perfection. I wasn't sure what perfection was, but I knew that God demanded it, and I didn't have it. That left me a little mad at God. How dare He provide a banquet that was not for me?

"Not for Me" became my theme song. Not for me the joy of fellowship. I was too shy. Not for me the comfort of acceptance. I was too far from perfect. Not for me the delight of participation. I had no talents. God had His favorites, and I was not one of them. My name was not on the guest list.

But God had no intention of leaving me placeless. My welcome was tucked away in the pages of His Book. There, principle upon principle and precept upon precept, I found my name correctly spelled and clearly marked. I was invited, expected, and would be fed!

When I first started studying the Bible, it made very little sense to me. I tried ploughing through it book by book, assuring myself that I was being richly blessed because this was God's message to me.

Somewhere in Leviticus, I gave up pretending and faced God with my problem. "Dear Lord," I said, "I know every word of this Book has a message to me from You. I thank You for that, but at the moment, I'm missing it. I am now in Leviticus, and I know exactly what to do if my neighbor's ox falls into a ditch. However, I live on the eighth floor of a high rise, and although I have suspected that my neighbors on the floor above me have an ox—should it fall into a ditch there would be very little I could do about it! If You want me to get Your message out of all these ancient truths, You'll have to open the Word to me in a special way."

A few weeks later, I was on my way to an audition. I was waiting at a bus stop when a sudden rainstorm began gullying the streets. I ran to a nearby bookstore for shelter. The rain got worse, and the bookstore closed. The sales clerk invited me to wait out the rain in an adjacent auditorium. When I learned that a missionary meeting was being held there, I refused. I knew I would not be interested in that.

I stepped outside and stood under a small awning, hoping that the rain would diminish. Then they rolled up the awning! I felt like Jonah under the gourd. (*See* Jonah 4:6.)

I ran into the auditorium and perched in the back row. I never took off my coat or put down my purse. I was not interested in the meeting. I only wanted to get out of the storm.

As I sat in the back of that auditorium in New York, I heard Major Ian Thomas speak of the objects within the Ark of the Covenant. I knew very little about the Ark of the Covenant and had given no thought to the meaning of its contents. To me, any such topic related to blackboard drawings in Sunday-school class. The Old Testament was a collection of unrelated stories about lackluster people in striped bathrobes—wonder workers who had no more to do with my world than the shadow of an airplane falling across the path of an ant.

But then as I sat in that New York auditorium, the clipped British phrases of Major Thomas introduced me to the living, human drama of the Bible as an account of the imperfect people through whom a perfect God worked out His perfect plan. I was faced with a new consideration.

I realized after that meeting that the problem was not in the Book, but in my approach to it. I had tried to approach it scientifically, philosophically, moralistically, although I was not a scientist, philosopher, or moralist—I was an actress. For the first time, I began to consider the Bible in the same way I would consider a script.

My initial acting approach is to examine the character of the role I am to play for any hint of me. I look for any identification I can use. This is my point of entry into the character—the point at which the character I play is most like my own character.

Using this method of study, I began to explore the living incidents of the Bible. I inquired into the lives of productive people of God. I found real men and women, who claimed the heights and depths of good and evil. I found that these created beings, whom God called friends, were not unlike me.

I learned that David cried all night, remembering some stupid choice he had made during the day. I have done that! I read that Jacob plotted and schemed for things his own greed had initiated. I have done that! Moses participated in a rash act he thought would be pleasing to the Lord and went through discipline because of it. I have done that! Eve thought God would move at the speed of her assumed timetable. I have done that! My Bible heroes did not have marbled toes on golden pedestals, but feet of clay. And yet, *they ran.*

I tore away my sanctimonious picture of the saints and found revelation. It was not the messengers who were perfect; it was the message. That first principle transferred me from a seat in the bleachers to a bench in the locker room. The parade of perfection had a break in the ranks that even I could enter.

There are many excellent books written from the viewpoint of a scientist or philosopher or forceful debater—this is not one. I don't offer the life story of a powerful saint or the scholarly thinking of a theologian. I can't run with them. This will be a book written out of my own experiences.

Some
Run With
Feet of
Clay

1
The Starting Line

Dear Lord,

Thank You for giving me the appetite and opportunity for writing a book. I praise Your name because I know You never call me to do anything You have not already equipped me to do. I am trying to take action on that which I know, rather than that which I feel.

I thank You for Your promise that You will complete what You have begun. On the basis of that promise, I know the battle of the book is already won and that You are indeed the victor.

However, there is one little problem. I do not know how to begin the book! Never before have I realized just how blank a blank piece of paper is—and how long.

Lord, Your Book begins with such majestic ease. I don't ask for anything as mighty as that, but I would so appreciate it if You would solve the anagram of my thoughts and give me some kind of opening chapter.

I pray in the name of the Lord, Jesus Christ.

Amen.

Many years ago I was in an off-Broadway show with little success. The pitifully brief run of that play was preceded by a lengthy rehearsal, and during that time, I held the position of Equity deputy. I was elected to this office while I was out of the meeting getting a drink of water, and greeted the news of my election with the ecstasy of one being told of a dentist's call in reference to an impacted wisdom tooth.

I took my job very much to heart, despite my initial reluctance. Every morning I would check with every cast member to be sure they were receiving their benefits. However, every morning one bright-eyed ingenue always said *no*. She hadn't received her insurance forms, her complimentary tickets, or her notice of the next Equity meeting.

I began to write imploring letters to the front office. The honor of my assignment was at stake if I could not manage full benefits for this one fledgling.

I had to admit defeat one morning. "My dear, I don't know what they have done with your records. I'm going to go over to the office and check into this personally. Are you a junior or a senior member?"

"Of what?" she inquired. Then it hit me.

"Do you mean that I have been writing letters to our union office criticizing their lack of attention to a *nonmember's* needs? Why didn't you tell me you were not a member?"

"You never asked me."

I learned a great principle that day: Before you try to apply the benefits, check first into the relationship between the "benefiter" and the "benefitee." Since this book will be primarily about the joys and privileges of being a Christian, I'm going to write first about becoming a Christian.

So—to the nonbeliever whom this may concern: I want you to know first that you are loved, really loved.

I, for one, love you because you've read this far and are still with me. I have an especially tender empathy for you. I was as you are for longer than I have been as I am.

More importantly, God loves you, and has taken action on your behealf. If you were given this book by someone, you are loved by that person. If a Christian gave you this book, he was not trying to earn Brownie points with God, because none are given. You've been given this book because someone wants to share with you something that might lead you into your full potential.

Did you know that God purposes good things for you? Nobility of man is not man's idea, it's God's idea. That was hard for me to understand. I thought God was some kind of super critic, trying to keep me belittled, humiliated, and smothered by restrictions. I used to say I didn't want God to take over my life, because I didn't want to be a puppet.

It wasn't until a short time ago that I learned the believer is not the puppet. The nonbeliever is. We often overlook the fact that God can use the nonbeliever just as easily as He can use the believer. During Israel's exodus from Egypt, God used Pharaoh as well as Moses, but He used Pharaoh like dead wood, and Moses as a contributing participant.

My road from fear of God's authority to gratitude for His Sovereignty was a long, hard one. It doesn't offer a very exciting story, though. I thank the Lord for each detail of my testimony, but do find it one of the duller accounts in the family!

We are so indoctrinated to externals that we measure testimonies by experiential happenings. We ask God's mysteries to move within the aura of our personal sense of drama, so that we may be tantalized, traumatized, and even titillated into fellowship.

I have known hundreds of Christians to lose confidence in their own relationship with Christ just because their account of it did not measure up to someone else's. The devil would rather you do anything in the world except accept Jesus Christ as your Saviour, but once you have gone against his Satanic will and accepted Christ, then he shifts his efforts to another purpose—that of making you doubt the validity of that acceptance.

A testimony should be an attesting to the work of Jesus Christ. It is His action that implants the drama in the Christian experience. That drama unfolds in a story of relationship.

I've heard a lot of Christian testimonies that held startling and vivid accounts of life before the encounter with Jesus. My sharing of Christ in me turns naturally to what I have claimed of Him *this day;* that I still stand amazed in the Presence, that His personal revelation in the *now* triggers joy beyond words.

I grew up in a Christian home, for which I thank the Lord. My home environment introduced me to prayer and Bible study as naturally as our backyard introduced me to lightning bugs and stars. I didn't know until I went away to school that one *chose* to go to church—I thought the only choice was between the 8:00 or 11:00 A.M. services.

My parents gave me the indelible memory of their

own personal involvement in Christianity. My mother evidenced prayer by her active participation in it. I am sure she is praying for me today as she has prayed for me every day of my life.

My fondest memory of my father is of him sitting out on the back porch after supper, reading his Bible. Years later, when I would scorn every remnant of what I had called faith, I could not toss away the fact of what my parents believed. What they did affected me far more deeply than what they said I should do.

When I was twelve years old I walked down the aisle of our church behind my parents and accepted the God they recognized. My father had joined the church from another denomination, and he and I were baptized together.

The baptismal pool seemed awfully deep and the assembled congregation frighteningly large. The minister ushered my father into the water, and then me. I wasn't much at ease about following the Lord Jesus, but I knew nothing but good could come from following my Daddy. So there I was, a scared and dripping twelve-year-old, newly baptized into the faith of her father. And there I stood for about twenty-two years.

By the time I got to New York, I had already begun to show the marks of growing old before I grew up. I had been in three Broadway shows that folded before they got in—a sure mark of success. I was doing regular summer stock and off-Broadway work. I had a fine agent, and had done several top commercials. I was doing just what I had always wanted to do, and I was miserable!

The great tragedy in life is not in failing to get what you go after. The tragedy is getting it and finding out it wasn't worth the trouble! I was depressed.

It's embarrassing when you're depressed and the circumstances aren't. Society allows us only programmed emotions. Grieve only at funerals, rejoice only at parties, and be depressed only when pressure is visible.

I began to feel guilty and ashamed. What kind of ingrate was I, to go around feeling depressed when there were people in Outer Mongolia who were starving and cold. But happiness is not derived from comparison. I've never known a hangnail to hurt less because someone else had a ruptured appendix. In spite of this, people generally try to treat depression by applying compresses hot with other people's woes.

In the midst of my depression, a friend sent me a copy of the Phillips translation of the New Testament. I was not regularly reading the Bible at that time. I knew enough about it to disprove some of it in verbal confrontations with Christians who knew a mite less than I did. Armed with a reverent ignorance as to what the Bible said, I argued determinedly against its validity.

Still, I had a Bible which I treasured. It was a little white Bible, wrapped in cellophane. I always plopped it down on my dressing-room table each time I opened a show. My white Bible served the purpose of making my friends feel ill at ease, and when they referred to it, I related *that* to insidious persecution, and tightened the belt of my nobility.

Have you noticed how many girdles are badly mis-

placed halos? A halo at best is a chancy adornment—
some Christians suffer from migraine because they
put their halos on themselves and place them a trifle
low and very tight!

My little white Bible was very precious to me. I
never read it, but panicked if I couldn't find it. One
night I was taken backstage at the Metropolitan Opera
to meet Jerome Hines. We stood in the doorway of his
dressing room and chatted. I looked past him and saw
on his dressing table what to me was a shocking sight.
A great big, floppy Bible was *open* on the table! The
binding was torn, the pages were dog-eared, there
were markings all over it.

Well, I thought, they tell me Jerome Hines is such a
fine Christian, but he certainly doesn't respect his Bible! I've learned another principle since then: If your
Bible is in good shape, you're not!

I looked through the Phillips translation without
much interest when it arrived. Suddenly, one phrase
entered the atmosphere of my understanding, like that
first fireball re-entry of our space program.

> Don't let the world around you squeeze you
> into its own mould . . . .
>
> Romans 12:2 PHILLIPS

That's what I was doing! I was letting the world
around me form the pattern of my own self. I had been
trying to purchase acceptance by pretending to be
what anyone wanted me to be!

If I was expected to be sweet, I tried to be sweet. If I
was expected to be funny, or smart, I would try that,

too. I was scared to meet new people because I might not be able to be the person they would expect. I was terrified of being with large groups, because they might expect me to be different persons at one and the same time!

The worst horror of all was being alone with one person who might discover the dreadful secret that I wasn't anyone at all—I was nothing but a reflection!

I can't help but be a bit envious of people having nervous breakdowns now. It's so much easier for them than it was for me. I had mine before they were popular and had to have it in secret.

Today you can turn to someone in an elevator and say "I'm having a nervous breakdown," and hear the answer "Really? I had mine last summer."

I couldn't tell anyone that I wasn't the happy child I appeared to be. There was no way out. I had pretended so well I almost kept my secret away from me, but it was brought clearly into focus by that verse from the Bible. *Don't let the world form you—be!*

How could I be? I didn't have any me to be. Mine was a major identity crisis, because I didn't have any identity!

2
Who Is This Leader?

Dear Lord,

I have an appetite for clarity but not the technique. I have tried to be honest and specific, but I am not an honestly specific person. When I first stood up to teach in a classroom, I blurted out my whole year's lesson plan in the opening lecture. Maybe I've done that again?

I want to proceed with the accounting of the Christian walk, but my mind keeps going back to the fundamentals of birth. Could it be that I am so eager to get on with my plan that I'm reluctant to spend too much time with Yours?

Well, Lord, once again start with me. *Make me* to go in the way of Your law. *Make me* to type in the words of Your choice, and *make me* to write only of that glorifying to Your purposes.

In the name of the Lord, Jesus Christ.

Amen.

One day, still deeply depressed, I found another Bible verse that spoke to me:

Yet the proof of God's amazing love is this: that it was while we were sinners that Christ died for us.

Romans 5:8 PHILLIPS

I still don't know all the theological ramifications of that verse, but I know what I understood then of its validity. Jesus Christ died for me *knowing I was a sinner.* He knew me and loved me anyway.

He knew that I made and broke resolutions in one and the same breath. He knew that all the love I claimed to have for others was mostly fake. He knew that my seemingly gentle manner covered seething resentments and a constantly critical evaluation of others. He knew the times I lied and all the times I had denied and would deny Him. He knew the only authority I had ever recognized was one based on threat, yet He offered me authority based on love. And He took action on my behalf.

More than anything else, the principle in that verse meant that for the first time in my life I had a relationship that was secure—because Jesus Christ already knew all the disappointing truths about me, and had taken action to free me from their pattern.

One night, all alone in my fine, dissatisfying apartment, I cried out, "All right! Jesus Christ, whoever You are, You take over." Can you guess what happened next? Can you imagine the sudden peace and joy that I experienced? I can't, because it didn't happen that way for me!

The next morning I felt the same, looked the same, and made the disgusting observation that I was the same! I hoped someone would notice a startling difference and tried to glow, but I failed miserably.

Finally, I admitted to a friend that I had turned my life over to Christ but nothing had happened. She told me I didn't have enough faith, so I started going home a little early and trying to have faith.

I didn't know how it was done, but I suspected it was done with the eyebrow muscles, because that's the look people had when they talked about it. You know what I mean. That rolling up of the forehead and wide spacing of the eyes to give the appearance of joy. I tried it, I really did. I didn't have any more faith, but I sure did have a headache! Oh, I wanted to have some fine validating experience! How could I ever hope to be a sure-fire Christian without it?

Some of all that effort was fine, but most of it was just plain stupid. Christ in you *will* make a difference, but *He* does it!

Faith is a gift of God. It is not, never was, and never will be a product of man's best efforts. It is a gift.

Scripture taught me that Jesus Christ is the author and finisher of our faith—faith comes by hearing; by hearing the Word of God. God healed me by His Word and in His Word I learned why something really wonderful had happened when I turned my life over to Jesus Christ.

In contemplating the imperfection of God's heroic saints, one principle undergirds each study: We may hope to run with feet of clay because Jesus Christ is who He is, has done what He has done, is doing what He is doing, and will do what He will do.

Every assurance the Christian holds is securely rooted in the character of God. That's the reason the comfort of God is based on His faithfulness and not ours.

I believe that most of the multitude that rejects

Christ today does so from ignorance. We Christians haven't told the story clearly.

I was in New York for a massive evangelism program. We were all keyed up by the excitement of what was being done and by our eagerness to be part of it. I remember someone told us to use that opportunity to tell everyone about Christ. Well, I took that to heart! I flung fragments of testimony to people on buses, to taxi drivers, to elevator operators, even to someone who got the first of my message before the subway doors benevolently separated us. I pray that God will get help to those poor confused people who heard only my rumors of the facts of God. The message must be clear and complete.

Who Is He?

When Jesus Christ entered Jerusalem the Sunday before His death, He was greeted with great and noisy acclaim. The gestures offered by those who accompanied Him to the steps of the temple were not tokens of casual choice. The coats and palm leaves thrown in His path, the words chanted so gleefully, even the donkey bearing its noble burden, were all statements about His identity.

A parade gathers paraders, and the whole city of Jerusalem was alerted to a time and person of significance. The residents of Jerusalem gathered in eagerness as Christ's unrehearsed procession passed through the winding streets. The Bible says that all the city was moved and asked, "Who is this?"

Can't you imagine the murmur that would sweep through the city after such an event? Who is He? Some carpenter who has been preaching in the temple comes into the city and a multitude of people go wild. Who is He?

I have wondered over that question, just as Jerusalem did. That one question lies at the heart of the whole Christian message and separates Christianity from all religions.

The multitude in Jerusalem said that He was the prophet of Nazareth. The coats and palm leaves that lay in His path proclaimed Him victor and king. The chanted words from Psalms 118 and the donkey He rode proclaimed Him to be Israel's Messiah.

All the insults and abuses thrown at Him, from the manger in Bethlehem to the cross of Calvary, but no one ever confronted Him with facts that would have dismissed His claimed identity.

The Messiah of Israel would have to fulfill prophecies of the sacred writings. One slight deviation from the pattern prescribed in the law would have relegated Him to the growing group of imposters that made the same claim He made.

Jesus not only claimed a unique relationship with God, but He linked Himself with His pre-existence. He said, ". . . before there was an Abraham, I AM!" (John 8:58). He forgave sin, which was only God's prerogative, and brought the dead to life, which was only God's power.

The prophecies said the Messiah would be born in Bethlehem Ephrata. Four hundred years later, Mary, a pregnant Jewish virgin, and her husband Joseph left Nazareth to return to the city of Joseph's birth— Bethlehem Ephrata.

The prophecies said the child Messiah would sojourn in Egypt, come out of Nazareth, and be heralded by a forerunner. Mary and Joseph, threatened by Herod, fled to Egypt before returning to Nazareth, where their child grew to perfect manhood. He was proclaimed by John the Baptist to be the Lamb of God who takes away the sin of the world.

The prophet Daniel predicted the time of His coming. Jeremiah painted the manner of His personality. The Psalms spelled out His work and teaching. Isaiah 53 gave a meticulous description of His death.

I didn't know these facts, and what I didn't know was hurting me. I thought God was trying to enlist me to establish His kingdom. I didn't know His kingdom had been established before the creation of the earth!

I thought Christ was either a poverty-bred infant in a manger or a badly mistreated man dying on a cross. No one ever got it through to me that that seemingly vulnerable baby and that man suffering in death had power beyond my understanding.

Who is He? Judas Iscariot gave his final answer to that question as he joined Christ and the other disciples at their final Passover meal.

I can just hear Judas' sharp intake of breath as Christ presented to him the honor of being the first guest served at the Passover dinner. Christ, knowing all there was to know about Judas, still gave him one final chance. Scripture says that after Judas took the bread, Satan entered into him.

Judas made a choice, like the free moral agent God had allowed him to be. To Judas, Jesus Christ may well have been the gentlest man he had ever known—a teacher beyond compare—a character of exemplary honesty—a personality of fascinating uniqueness—but not God, self-functioning in His Sovereign right to unquestioned authority. Not God. Not Lord, to whom only obedience is reasonable and for whom no sacrifice is wasted. And for Judas, who chose to be beyond persuasion, He was not Saviour.

And then, knowing Judas had made his choice, Christ leaned forward and said, "What you are about to do—do at once!" The betrayed exercised His authority over the betrayer by prodding him into God's timetable. "Judas," Christ said, "you're late. Do it now!" Judas went out of there like a shot.

Not even the mockery of a mismanaged trial, or the agony of acute physical suffering wrested power from this man. After hours of torture, paid out second by second, He cried with the full strength of a loud voice, and by His still-authoritative power, He *gave up* His life. Who is He? Who is this One who calls forth the cues of His own betrayal and in His death, as well as in His birth, fulfills every prophecy?

What Has He Done?

He lived a perfect life that offered a scant three years of active ministry. He healed the sick, He forgave sins, He taught with shocking authority, He collected a little band of followers, and He offered His life as atonement for sin.

The life of Christ set many patterns for Christians, but it is His death that provides the means by which the example He gave can be followed. Our feet are fallible; only by His help can we walk in His steps.

He said He identified with man as man. He said He identified with God as God. He said He was willing to pay the price for the chasm in between. That's why He died. No one took Christ's life from Him. He gave it away. When Peter urged Him to detour Jerusalem and avoid the threat of death, Christ answered, "It was for this reason I came into the world!" The last words He spoke from the cross were uttered in full control of His senses.

Why was this special One literally born to die? Because God and man had been irrevocably separated by sin. God said He would redeem us from sin, deliver us out from under. That's a phrase from the Bible that eases me everytime I read it:

> . . . I will bring you out from under the burdens . . . .
>
> Exodus 6:6

God spelled out the only acceptable sacrifice for sin—that which would deliver us out from under. In the Book of Isaiah, the prophet offers a detailed account of the Messiah's sacrifice.

> . . . and the Lord hath laid on him the iniquity of us all.
>
> Isaiah 53:6

The iniquity of us all laid on Him! That's what was so totally finished on the cross. That's why Christ cried out, "It is finished." The full payment for sin rested upon Christ.

And in that moment, Christ, separated from God the Father by our sins, cried out, "My God, My God, why hast Thou forsaken me?" God can have no fellowship with sin, even when it is His only-begotten Son hanging there beneath sin's monstrous burden. That's what Christ did for us. Divine atonement. We accept that when we accept Him as Lord.

That's why I am a Christian. I exercised my choice for Christ, and that decision meant that all He was in His person and all He did to pay the price for my sin was credited to my account. As I identified with Him, His identification with me made me acceptable unto God, and valuable. I am a person of value because of the identity and work of Christ.

The Christian life begins when an individual faces the fact of his need for a Saviour and trusts Jesus Christ to meet that need. If you have never given your life over into the hands of Jesus Christ, you are still on the outside looking in, and you have no idea what the Christian life is all about.

Now is as good a time as any to put that matter in order. You can claim life everlasting right now. All you need say is: "Jesus Christ, I am a sinner, and I believe You died for me in my place. I take You as my Lord and Saviour. Thank You for saving me."

All the complexity has been taken care of by God, who loved you so much He has already done the hard part. You can't make Him any promises of your perfection, but you can trust His perfection to do *for* you, and then *in* you, all He promised *to* you.

3
Brave a New Beginning

Dear Lord,

Writing a book is a very disturbing experience. I am now realizing how little I know and how much I have been talking about it. Trying to put down on paper the words of my reflections makes me feel a stark sense of inadequacy.

There is so much of You I would like to tell people, particularly those tender-skinned newly born ones, who are just stepping out in the time of Your life. There is so much confusion handed out as spiritual instruction—I don't want to be just another midway barker touting a sideshow event. I want to offer positives and principles and, Oh Lord, how I want my book to be a new book.

I am so greedy! I don't want to say an old thing a new way. I want to say a new thing! Where this is an appetite glorifying to You, please open up ways for it to be satisfied. Where it is just another aspect of my own ego trying to look holy, please dismiss it. Please cram my barefooted thoughts into the shoes of Your discipline, that I might run effectively.

I pray in the name of our Lord, Jesus Christ.

Amen.

Most Christians testify to their early Christian experiences with terms only slightly less rhapsodic than those describing true millennial joy. There is a lilting account of exuberant security, welcoming fellowship, unbounded love, and instant maturity. If this has been your experience in the Lord, I honestly praise His name for His dealings with you and ask your patient indulgence for my account of a different experience.

My newly committed life was one of disturbing, even though sanctified, confusion. I knew more fears, more self-doubt, and more irritation than I had ever known. I made more serious errors in my first few weeks as a proclaiming Christian than I had in my whole history of unabashed carnality!

One of the surest proofs of the invincibility of Christianity is that it survived my first five years of active involvement! Instead of leaping daintily in gazellelike surefootedness, I stumbled two steps backward for every three steps forward.

I felt no sense of direction and no clearly defined purpose. My feelings of joy were as changeable as my testimony, which knew daily adjustments to the circumstances under which I was to give it.

As for love, that highly touted affection that was supposed to drench my new being, I found no honest indication of it, either from me or to me. My new Christian friends welcomed me into the family with terms and tones I didn't understand, which reminded me of a particularly confusing phase of my actual childhood.

I was the only child of parents who came from large families. We were the only branch of either lineage which did not live in its native environs of Alabama or Oklahoma. As a result, I grew up thinking Christmas meant Alabama and Thanksgiving meant Oklahoma, because that was when and where the clans gathered.

I felt that *family* meant a house full of strangers bearing not only gifts, but kisses and hugs and double names all beginning with aunt, uncle, or cousin. The most impressive names were those that bore variations sounding like physical phenomena: "This is your second cousin once removed," or "This is your fourth cousin on your mother's side." I visualized cousins hanging like appendages to my parents' history and wondered why I was supposed to love these vaguely familiar creatures.

Family-type people talked a lot about incidents that were strange to me. Family-type people were often excited about special events that occurred in that mysterious time before I was born. I became convinced that I had entered the scene after the best part was over, but felt I had gotten myself born at the earliest possible opportunity and resented any feeling of guilt on account of my tardiness. None of this put me at ease.

False Start

My response to my Christian family was much the same. I was slow in picking up their phrases and embarrassed that the accent of my old way of life colored my speech. There is a hymn that includes the phrase, "Jesus calls us o'er the tumult." Well, I had difficulty in hearing the clear voice of Jesus over the tumult of the Christian community!

God's plan and direction are usually quite simple, but we Christians are wonderfully imaginative. If we can find a way to complicate God's plan, we are not only willing to do it, we are also eager to teach others those complications. I feel great sympathy for the spiritual fledgling trying to piece together God's guidance from the feverish counsel of those of us advising him.

Years ago, as my ears were bombarded by phrases, my newly committed heart was not warmed. I longed for love to happen to me, even while I tried to deal with my very active resentment. Why was no one interested in the things that interested me? And, if God really loved me, why had He told everyone else exactly what I should do and not revealed a whiff of direction to me personally?

I was urged to get into a church, join in a fellowship, and spend a significant part of my busy mornings in quiet time. I tried an early morning quiet time, only to find it considerably quieter than expected. Napping with my nose pressed into an open Bible was not honestly productive!

Following my usual pattern of rejecting what I did not understand, I fought each suggested principle, and lived to regret each battle.

I substituted self-gratifying daydreaming for prayer. I found the Bible dull and confusing in the few haphazard attempts I made at study, so I eliminated that practice. I considered myself above the need for church involvement because my relationship with Christ was unique.

Having dispensed with the organized church, I moved on to check off the whole Christian community. I didn't need any of them. I was secure in the

Lord. He would lead me, and the straitlaced Christians could eat my dust as I zoomed past them.

I did not zoom ahead, however—I skidded across the track and almost out of the race. I didn't know what hurt me. I was lonely without spiritual fellowship and totally unequipped for the battle I found myself fighting.

Yes, a real battle! There is a mighty conflict still going on. Satan, who fought so hard to keep the Christian from becoming a Christian, will fight even harder to render the Christian ineffective. I learned the truth of Galatians 5:17 before I ever read the verse. The flesh *is* at war with the Spirit. I needed help. I was taking myself right out of the race, almost before it began!

Realizing I was floundering into defeat by trying to live the Christian life all by myself, I went back to the dynamics of honest prayer, back to the vulnerability of real fellowship. I learned that I could hear the deep, God-based love in my Christian family when I stopped stiff-arming everyone with criticism. I was about to set my foot upon the hallowed ground of true beginnings.

Tentative Steps

When we relish the authenticity of our own personhood under God, we allow the authenticity of others. That's the beginning place—the authenticity of the person whom Christ has created.

If any man be in Christ he is a newly created being . . . .

See 2 Corinthians 5:17

That's the challenge: risking all on the validity of God's bequest of personal identity. It is a risk. There would be no victory without the possibility of defeat. The action of life must begin in a world where loss is possible.

There are a lot of frustrated Christians who are left stranded in the delivery room because the great generative power of God has not been applied to the first timid steps of beginnings.

When I was in high school, one of the few group activities approved by teenager and parent alike was ice skating. Winter in Texas amounted to only a slight chill in our December sunbathing, but the ice-skating rink offered us a glimpse of winter, synthetic as it was. I loved it!

It was all very colorful and romantic. The blaring recorded music drenched us with melody as the lights on the rink changed to various moods.

True to my role of class clown, I hobbled down the steps to the ice, arms flailing the air in exaggerated precariousness, my weak ankles teetering back and forth over the slender blades.

Once upon the ice, I abandoned myself to the heights of my skating ambition—not to fall down. In order to satisfy this challenge, I spent my time skimming the edge of the rink, crossing hand over hand along the rail.

Following this procedure for all my skating dates and parties, I realized my one ambition—I *never* fell down. My friends flitted across the ice. The boys etched deep, icy patterns with their skates, while girls twirled and posed. They called out to me to join them.

I never left my course. They might be having more fun, but they had to fall down every once in a while. My record was perfect! No skating, no falling!

Sooner or later, the Christian realizes his heavenly Father did not fit him out just to learn the route along the rail. Sooner or later we are affected by the external goal expressed in the joy of other Christians, and by the internal goad of the Holy Spirit.

We don't want to give up going to the rink, so we ask, "Where do I go from here?" God has an honest answer. It requires that we brave a new beginning.

4
Elisha—Running His Own Race

Dear Lord,

You don't have to go out of Your way to remind me of the way beginnings feel. I remember as though it were yesterday. In fact, it's closer than yesterday—it's right now.

Deal first with my own fears, Lord, that I might offer some answers to the fears of others. I know I carry no other responsibility than availability to You, but my mind keeps wandering off to some unknown reader I so earnestly want to please.

I confess I am more concerned with that reader's relationship to this book than I am with my relationship to You. If it is at all possible, I would like to hold the attention of you both, but if the choice is either/or, I hereby shift my priorities to Your direction. However, dear Lord, if You are concerned about the same reader who concerns me, please give me the words to keep that reader reading.

I pray in the name of the Lord, Jesus Christ.

Amen.

Elisha, a great prophet of Israel, lived about 850 years before Christ. The son of a prosperous farmer, he was called by God into a ministry containing more recorded miracles than that of any other Old Testament prophet.

Elisha stood firmly against the pagan culture of his time and was a channel of blessings from God Almighty to a multitude of sufferers. His life shines with a special significance, but once he stood facing an audience of critics, a raw, untried beginner on the wrong side of the Jordan River, in a secondhand coat.

Elisha's Casting

Casting calls are the most draining experiences actors can have. When people tried to dissuade me from going into professional theater, they told me how hard the work was. They should have threatened me with realistic accounts of how hard the waiting would be: waiting backstage, waiting during rehearsals, waiting for call-backs, waiting for agents—endless waiting! Worst of all is the waiting in hundreds of outer offices for initial interviews and readings that might just possibly mean waiting for work.

Elisha's casting was of an entirely different nature. The casting agent called him! Elisha was hard at work in his father's fields when Elijah gave him the job.

> So he departed thence, and found Elisha the
> son of Shaphat, who was plowing with twelve
> yoke of oxen . . . and Elijah passed by him, and
> cast his mantle upon him.
>
> 1 Kings 19:19

There's an interesting principle in that verse. Elisha was not off somewhere, waiting in idleness for a bolt from the blue. I am really impressed by how many of God's heroic servants were called while they were busily applying themselves to the task at home.

My mother tells of spending a long day at the doctor's office, taking those dreary tests that are generally worse than the illness for which they are testing. At the end of the day, as everyone was finishing the day's records, one of the dressing room doors burst open, and a rather large man, draped in a rather small smock, bellowed at the amazed office workers, "When is someone going to get to me?"

Do you ever feel like that? I do! When is God going to get to me? Has He forgotten me? Noah may have wondered that as he waited for over a year in an ark full of undiapered animals! Have you figured that since God didn't honor your plan and your timing, He had no more use for your person?

Sometimes ignoring our plan is the best thing God can do for us, and sometimes delaying our plan is the most protective thing He can do for us. Wait for God's plan. He didn't forget Elisha. He won't forget you.

Be at ease and be productive, wherever you are as you wait. God remembers where He placed you. He knows just where to look when the time comes to call you.

> And he left the oxen, and ran after Elijah, and said, Let me, I pray thee, kiss my father and my mother, and *then* I will follow thee . . . .
>
> 1 Kings 19:20

Elisha was also deeply aware of the earnestness of commitments. He came into the Lord's service with full understanding of cause and effect.

We Christians have mistreated the spontaneity of our Sovereign God. He has every right to call us with our hand on the plow, or with a roast in the oven, or with cruise tickets in our pocket. He has every right to call us to anything, anytime He chooses. But He is, was, and always will be, a God of order. Being a God of order and discipline, He wants us to learn the meaning of commitment. Sometimes we must learn it by sticking to some tedious job we accepted by mistake. God's call carries the accent of integrity, and there is no integrity in a contract casually broken.

Elisha had learned the meaning of commitment. He applied himself wholeheartedly to the task assigned, and before he left home for a new task, he carried out his responsibilities to his family. He loved his home, even as he left it!

> And he returned back from him, and took a yoke of oxen, and slew them, and boiled their flesh with the instruments of the oxen . . . .
>
> 1 Kings 19:21

As Elisha was preparing a banquet for his family and friends, he dispensed with the instruments of his past occupation. The Lord who gives us grace to serve also gives us grace to sever. Elisha claimed God's grace to sever as well as to serve.

What a lesson that was for me! The old ways are so comfortable, the old ties are tender, the paths that are known rub the feet so gently. Some of us live our whole lives in small alcove attachments to the security of our childhood, afraid to deal with more than the shadow of maturity. Elisha moved forward into the area of his assignment. He responded with joy to that which was set before him and fulfilled with devotion the honor of his past.

He offered a banquet celebration to share in the joy of his new calling. I hope Elisha had the kind of family that celebrated with him. I hope he had parents who were willing to release their child to the maturity they had prepared him to have.

Elisha's background trained him to plow, but God called him to preach. Sometimes it is hard for us who are ready for the plowing to celebrate the call to preaching. Perhaps Elisha's show of responsibility, his consistency, and his willingness to part with his old occupation made it easier for his family to celebrate. They must have seen in those actions the maturity that meant he was ready to move out on his own—under God.

> Then he arose, and went after Elijah, and ministered unto him.
>
> 1 Kings 19:21

Elisha's Rehearsal

God not only equips us to do everything He calls us to do, He also gives us ample time for rehearsal. Opportunities for training always precede His opportunities for performance.

Apparently Elisha had about ten years of coaching from his master Elijah. Ten years of seeing Elijah's ministry as prophet and teacher. Ten years of learning from his example as well as from his instruction. I am sure those years were rich in meaning, although occasionally rough in method. Good teachers are not always gentle teachers.

A good teacher is a rare gift of God. It is so much easier to win friends than it is to teach students. A true teacher purposes to teach and leaves the popularity contests to others.

Elisha had the benefit of a great teacher, Elijah: a teacher who committed himself to preparing his student for a significant ministry. Elisha accepted the discipline of that preparing.

I learned the lesson about the need for preparation the hard way! One night I was on my way to teach a Bible class for which I was not prepared. On the way to the class, I prayed fervently that God would use that class to His glory in spite of my limitations.

God honored my prayer in a mighty way. It was one of the most-productive classes I had ever taught. I thanked the Lord for His last-minute deliverance and was very grateful that *He* had had such a good lesson all prepared.

The next teaching assignment, the same thing happened. It was wonderful. I thought I had discovered a new and definitely liberating principle!

My next week's booking was in California and included the presentation of a Bible monologue and a twenty-minute address. I flew out with a light heart—I did not prepare my talk or concern myself with the assignment. I knew God would take care of all the details.

I was so at ease! As I walked out to the platform I felt no tension, no concern, no touch of apprehension.

I knew the Lord would bail me out in a spectacular way!

I was introduced and walked to the microphone, still trusting God to provide words and a text at the last minute. He didn't! Seven times I thanked the audience for having me there, while I waited for revelation! Nothing! Finally, after what seemed like hours, I said, "As David says in the Psalms . . . ." quoted two *proverbs*, and sat down.

I couldn't believe it! God had left me up there, unprepared. That's when I learned another principle: God was not going to pull miracles out of the hat just to cover my lack of preparedness. If I valued His assignment, I would commit myself to my homework as a part of my ministry. He gave me time to get ready for His opportunity, and He would hold me accountable for it.

That's what rehearsals are for. Amateurs cling to the idea that good theater springs from that mystical period between a dreadful rehearsal and a magnificent opening night. Professional actors (and great prophets) are more apt to expect a satisfying progression from rehearsal to rehearsal, as actors and director work together toward a good performance.

5
Elisha at the Jordan

Dear Lord,

Well, it's started. I am now more eager to write than I am to write well. I don't know whether that's good or bad. I only know that my "vaulting ambition," as Shakespeare calls it, can throw a body block to my spontaneity. I keep wanting everyone to like me, my work, my book.

Even while I write about the all-sufficiency of Your grace, I keep plotting for means of personal gratification not necessarily of Your grace!

Last night Cliff Barrows taught me a new meaning for an old verse, and I claim it this morning. ". . . bringing into captivity every thought to the obedience of Christ . . ." (2 Corinthians 10:5).

I take the thought of my own ambition for this book and by my choice place it under the domination of obedience to You. I give You the right to my every whim, thought, or purpose. You can use that as a goad for my typing fingers, as a delay in my progress, or as a blocking of my intentions.

In the name of the Lord, Jesus Christ.

Amen.

Elisha and Elijah worked well together as teacher and student, master and servant, prophet and protégé. Then came the time for final dress rehearsals.

For those of you who do not know the experience of theater, let me make you aware of the sodden signifi-cance of dress rehearsals. At best they are organized confusion; at worst they are not to be described at all!

It is at dress rehearsal that you learn that all levels are higher, entrances longer, steps steeper, and changes shorter than they were simulated to be. You hope to learn these things at dress rehearsal, because if you learn them at a later date you are in serious trouble.

Elisha's dress rehearsal is described in 2 Kings 2. The master Elijah, in preparing for his departure, conducted a farewell tour of all the seminaries he had established in Israel. Elisha followed him, although he was given the opportunity to turn back at every stop.

Each new trial toward getting a show on is another opportunity to quit. Finally wearing fatigue like an oversized coat, your whole being glistening with the blistered sunburn of nervousness, all your doubts and anxieties exposed by the stage manager's tap on your dressing-room door, you learn that the final challenge is just to endure. Not to leave town, not to fake laryn-gitis, not to have a tantrum and cancel the show, but to be there—win, lose, or draw. To be there!

Elisha firmly told Elijah, "I'm staying!"

The seminarians were quick to question Elisha as to the wisdom of following a lame duck prophet. "Don't you know," they said, "that your master will be leav-ing you today?"

I can imagine Elisha's tone of voice when he an-swered all those questions. "Believe me, I know. Just keep quiet! I'm dealing with it."

Finally they came to the Jordan River. This is always a place marking a decision—a place of ultimate choice. With fifty of the students watching,

> . . . Elijah took his mantle, and wrapped it together, and smote the waters, and they were divided hither and thither, so that they two went over on dry ground.
>
> 2 Kings 2:8

> And it came to pass, when they were gone over, that Elijah said unto Elisha, Ask what I shall do for thee, before I be taken away from thee . . . .
>
> 2 Kings 2:9

"What do you want of me, Elisha? I've taught you, coached you, directed you, encouraged you, criticized you. What else can I do for you?"

I imagine Elisha could almost hear the opening strains of the overture as he answered, because he asked for the one thing he needed: power for his ministry. Not for a star on his dressing-room door, not for a full-page ad in *Variety*, not for a run-of-the-show contract, but for *power for the task assigned.*

Elijah replied, "If you see me go, you have it."

> And it came to pass, as they still went on, and talked, that, behold, there appeared a chariot of fire, and horses of fire, and parted them both asunder; and Elijah went up by a whirlwind into heaven. And Elisha saw it, and he cried,

My father, my father, the chariot of Israel, and
the horsemen thereof. And he saw him no more:
and he took hold of his own clothes, and rent
them in two pieces. He took up also the mantle
of Elijah that fell from him, and went back, and
stood by the bank of Jordan.

2 Kings 2:11–13

The dress rehearsal was over.

Elisha's Opening Night

The fifty seminarians filed into their seats in the
audience, waving at one another, rattling their programs, and checking their ticket stubs. Yes, the audience was all assembled. Fifty of them, over there
across the Jordan.

"Isn't this the show that Elijah made famous?"

"Yes, this boy studied under him. But I hear he can't
touch him in the part."

"Well, an Elijah comes along once in a generation. I
don't see why this young fellow is going to try to do
Elijah's act."

I can tell you why: He had to! He was on the wrong
side of the Jordan—his ministry was on the other side.

This is the place where you and I watch Elisha's
footprints for help as to where our steps should go.
The house lights dim. The curtain opens. The scene is
set. Elisha enters!

That in itself takes a lot of nerve. He strides right to
the middle of the stage, where everyone can see him.
He takes his place right at the banks of the river Jordan. He lifts that old wrinkled coat of Elijah's over the
waters and speaks his first line: "Where is the Lord

God of Elijah?" (2 Kings 2:14).

Have you been there? Did you exercise your choice to accept the call to service? Did you give your agreement to the Lord and sever the bonds that held you to your past? Did you study and seek for that which would prepare you for your mission?

Did you prepare and purpose and pray and practice—and forget that someday you, all by yourself, would have to perform? I did. When I stood at the point of beginning, I was too surprised to wave the mantle!

There is really nothing like the first time you are in front of an audience. There are other kinds of terror, in performances much greater, but none quite like that first experience. One year, the After Dinner Players (a Christian drama group) opened a show with a young man who had never been on the stage before. Early in the play he had a brief line, securely tucked in between the lines of our more seasoned troupers. He was very casual about the whole thing and enjoyed rehearsals and all the preparation time.

Opening night he was very much at ease. He thanked the Lord and each of us for the opportunity of being with the Players in this show. As director, I make a special point of leaving the stage area and watching all opening performances from the back of the audience, so I had an excellent view of our young actor's debut.

He walked out on stage with the group, smiling pleasantly and in character. He did very well until he happened to glance out toward the audience. We had prepared him for every contingency—except the fact that there would be people in the seats. He saw them. His eyes widened. His whole body swayed forward, as if drawn by a magnet in the front row. Then he swayed back, with his jaw dropped—still smiling—and his body tensed into unnatural quiet.

I thought he was going to faint, but he didn't faint, he didn't move. When the time came for his line, he didn't speak. He just gazed at the audience in open-mouthed amazement at their presence.

The actors on either side of him covered his one line and prodded him gently from time to time to move him about the stage. Somewhere in the second five minutes he seemed to thaw, just as suddenly as he had frozen, and he completed the show as rehearsed.

Elisha must have known something of that feeling. He must have known that sudden appraisal of one's own capacity that sends up a flat negative. Let's consider a few questions God may have answered for Elisha, who faced his first performance at the Jordan.

"Why can't I swim across?" You can, but if God planned you to walk it, you might drown by swimming. God has you there for a purpose. He wants you to learn something and He wants to teach through you at the same time. Life is filled with a lot of adjustments that we have to make. Don't start out with one that isn't necessary. Try to walk it—that's why you and everyone else are here.

"Could we have another quick rehearsal?" This is one of those things that can't be helped by another rehearsal. Besides, now is the time for you to learn one of the greatest principles a performer ever learns: Trust the rehearsals you have had! More importantly,

you've been working under an absolutely perfect Director-Producer. He has never had an error in His timing, and He never will. When He says you are ready for the show, believe Him, you are!

"How did Elijah do that?" Elisha smote the waters just as Elijah did, the waters parted, just as they did for Elijah, but this time *Elisha* went over. The waiting audience applauded because they saw the spirit of Elijah rested on Elisha. It was Elisha's ministry that waited on the other side. It was not Elijah's trick that got Elisha across the river, but the work of the God of Elijah through Elisha.

Elisha on His Own

Soon after I became active in outspoken Christianity, I met a lovely Christian leader who has become one of my dearest friends. Her name is Marge Caldwell, and I know of few women who have accomplished more unto the glory of the Lord.

I heard her speak and saw the reaction and immediately assumed that that was what a Christian speaker was supposed to be. I tried to be just like her. I laughed like she does, I copied her approach to an audience, and I even told her jokes. It was terrible! I was miserable, my audiences were miserable, and I'm sure if Marge had seen me, she would have been miserable!

I went limping back to the Lord. I explained to Him that I had tried my best to be like Marge and wanted to know where I had gone wrong. The Lord let me know He had a Marge, and she was doing a fantastic job of being Marge. However, He did have an empty space on His team. He didn't have anyone being Jeannette.

It was difficult for me to deal with the fact that my own personhood—created by Christ, grasped by Christ, maintained by Christ—was important to the plan of Christ. I was startled to learn from Scripture that Christ loved me in my own being. Instead of teaching me to be just like someone else, He is teaching me the technique of my full personal potential: the technique of my own authenticity.

God will go to any lengths to get us to trust Him so we will risk being ourselves. He'll call us, prepare us, teach us, direct us. He'll whisk away our Elijahs, that we might stand at the riverbank alone and begin the greatest adventure of them all: Being ourselves under God's authority.

> . . . and when he also had smitten the waters, they parted hither and thither: and Elisha went over.
>
> 2 Kings 2:14

Elisha's feet had to find their own path for his beginnings. He had to step out in his personal authenticity under the creative authority of God.

My personal authenticity is a gift from God, but I claim it only as I move out in instant obedience and constant availability to Him who made my authenticity valid. That is why we must first be obedient in the small, frequently tedious details of God's directives.

That is why the grandeur of what may be our ministry frequently depends on our willingness to submit to the discipline of Bible study, the dependence of prayer, and the structure of fellowship. Those are God's directives. Acceptance of them is reliance on God's preparation for our performance at the Jordan.

Elisha learned that lesson before the waters parted. He stood with a secondhand coat and a first-hand assignment and took action in obedience and availability unto the Lord. He had crossed the Jordan the first time as the servant of Elijah, but he crossed back as the servant of the living God.

What about that critical audience? When they saw Elisha strolling across the river, they recognized the One whom he served. They gave him a kneeling ovation.

> . . . they said, The spirit of Elijah doth rest on Elisha. And they came to meet him, and bowed themselves to the ground before him.
>
> 2 Kings 2:15

In the next chapter I'll talk about failure, because all reviews aren't good, but this audience saw the personhood of Elisha and recognized the Personhood of God.

6
The Hurdle of Depression

Dear Lord,

I remember one morning I was to speak to the chapel at Baylor University. I was afraid that morning, so I began to pray. "Lord, give me a verse of comfort to free me from my fears."

You have never spoken to me in an audible voice, Lord, but I do hear You in Scripture. You spoke to me that morning, clearly. You answered, "Sanctify the Lord of hosts himself; and let him be your fear . . ." (Isaiah 8:13).

I thought You hadn't answered me. "But Lord, I asked You to take away my fears, and You've given me a new one. How about another verse?"

I was wrong, of course. When I properly establish the priorities of fear, I strive only to please You, I am then released from the panic of punishment and disciplined by the productivity of Your direction. Thank You, Lord.

I pray in the name of the Lord, Jesus Christ.

Amen.

The other day I called one of the most productive Christians I know. "How are you?" I asked, thinking it was a somewhat needless question. She was always fine, and had nineteen Scripture verses to prove it!

I didn't get her usual answer, though. Instead I got a

long pause, and then words all capsulated in one breath.

"Oh, Jeannette, I'm awful! I've been so depressed I don't know what to do. I've had to quit teaching my Bible classes. I'm not doing anything. I don't go out, I don't see anybody. It's all I can do just to get up in the morning, and some days I can't even do that. I'm so ashamed of myself I don't think I can stand it!"

This was no erratic spiritual novice; this was a mighty Christian soldier! I had seen her in action and praised God for her accuracy as she taught or counseled. My heart hurt for her. This dear friend was not only down in the depths, but ashamed of herself for being there.

I became very clinical. "Are you eating a lot of sugar? Are you overtired? Are you taking sulfa drugs?" She seemed taken aback by my questions, but I have learned there are many different reasons for depression, and some of them are physical.

Then I asked my friend about the condition of her prayer life—was she aware of hidden resentment? of disobedience? There was nothing that surfaced before my considerably less-than-professional eye, and I decided to doff my counselor's cap for the more likely bonnet of a friend.

How we love to grip the believer's spiritual pulse with our untrained fingers and rattle off our diagnosis. Then, as patients, we frequently offer far more curiosity as to what the disease is than in how to cure it. That's why some books have become best sellers— they tell people the names of their ailments. If naming it is curing it, there would be no need for drugstores!

I wonder if all the justified popularity of lay coun-
seling has endangered some of the basics of our spon-
taneous feelings for one another. We don't *talk* anymore, we "Communicate." We never *tell* somebody
something, we "Share." We react from our study man-
uals instead of from our hearts. Sometimes we become
so sure of the text on relationship that we've missed
the context of honest contact.

God forgive me the times I've cheated my friends,
trying to satisfy some imagined assignment rather than
be myself! That's a trap satanically laid for a lot of
public speakers. We are so used to handing out services we forget to be *fellow* servants. I hate to think of
the times I have doled out advice and dispassionate
counsel when what was asked of me was love and
prayers!

Fortunately, my house has a smoothly running
thermostat designed to correct such false temperature
readings. It is called a husband. Someone asked me
how I managed to survive the sudden popularity that
followed *The Hiding Place,* and I answered without
hesitation: "Lorraine."

Even with his masterful understanding, it is often
very difficult. After having listened attentively to the
needs of disturbed strangers, I am prone to counsel
my own husband, who neither needs nor appreciates
it!

I thought of this as I sympathized with my depressed friend on the telephone. She had not inadver-
tently gotten her line crossed with "Dial-an-analyst,"
she was admitting a painful condition to a friend. I
think the most helpful thing I offered her was that I

was not shocked. Surprised a little, but not shocked.

Any Christian who is truly shocked by another Christian's depression has not dealt honestly with the possibility of her own. I was no more shocked than I am when I learn that a friend has hay fever. Depression is a lot like hay fever—almost everyone has it, but no one knows what to do about it.

After sharing tears with my friend, I did offer two quick dispensings of advice. I am not a professional counselor and do not hesitate to recommend one when I think it is needed, but I feel two principles offer successful first aid to depression-suffering Christians. They may even be the cardinal rules for survival.

Principle one: Depression is temporary! If you are subject to attacks of depression, tape a sign to your closet door, or embroider it onto the pillow into which you cry. *It is temporary—do not make any long-term decisions under the influence of a short-term condition!*

The well-quoted lady who always bought a new dress whenever she was depressed must have a closet full of hideous clothes, all reminding her of her depression! Depression is indeed real. It is tragic. It is paralyzing, it is contagious, it is every horrible thing you may imagine it to be, but it is temporary! The devil would have you believe that depression is permanent, eternal, unique, and that there is no way out from under it. Those are all lies! Refute them— between your tears, if you must—but refute them.

Principle two: Depression is redeemable. God never wastes anything. He is the Glorious Scavenger!

If released to Him, every tear, every sob, every shudder of shaking shoulders can be productive!

I knew my friend's tears had not left their moist tracks on hours that were beyond God's attention. God knows the worth of our weepings. Think about that the next time you're crying. God knows just how many tears come from a broken and contrite heart (and how many do not!). The fact of God's unfaltering economy of suffering has done me more good than waterproof mascara.

After talking to my friend, I found myself thinking a lot about depression, especially in the life of the believer, who may have thought it disproved the belief. The believer in Christ has a means of dealing with depression victoriously, but he certainly is not immune to it.

The trickiest point for the depressed Christian is that someone with a handsome face but a demonic accent told him to say nothing about it and it would go away. The Christian is never depressed, no sir! The Christian is a happy fellow. See how he smiles. See how he prays for those less fortunate ones who know downs instead of ups. See him give his testimony. See him cut his throat!

If you are not a Christian, or are a very new one, you may be put off by my friendly reference to depression. Even if it is bad psychology to introduce a discouraging word here on the fringe of your birthday party, believe me, the principles of overcoming frustration, guilt, and disappointment will do you far more good than all the left-over paper hats.

On the other hand, if you are a Christian with time

accredited to your record, you may be delighted by this chapter. It may even be that you have just tripped in your joyous running and are now lying face down in the mire of unfulfilled commitments to righteousness. You may have seen all the saints passing you by without giving you a second glance and wondered why none of those loving brethren saw fit to warn you of the true conditions of the track!

At this point, you may have convinced yourself that you really don't want to run anyway, and that the roadside gutter is a lot like a fiftieth birthday—once you get over the shock of it, it's really not so bad.

Well, friend, there's good news and bad news. The bad news is that God has no intention of allowing you to adjust to the gutter, no matter how rough it is getting back in the running. The good news is that God has already done the hard part and provided you with principles to get you going again. Those principles were carried out by noble characters who faltered long before you.

If the tour guide points out all the homes of the track stars, you'll find three of special interest. They are not exactly homes—they're tents. Each one is different, but all three are definitely off the track.

One is a little smaller than the others, and has certain touches here and there of femininity. The usual basic tent flap is adorned by fading embroidered curtains, the tent itself is pink, with matching poles. It is a lady's tent. A lovely lady named Hannah, whose feet longed to dance even though they were hobbled by clogs designed only for walking. Hannah stumbled in frustration.

The middle tent is quite ornate. It is made of purple velvet, appropriately weatherproofed, adorned with the woven gold insignia of a king—a very great king. David, the king of Israel, whose marching feet found the deadly detour of guilt.

The far one under the juniper tree is made of coarse heavy material that looks like sackcloth, the rough cloth of a prophet. It belongs to Elijah, whose leaping path is marked by prints slimy with disappointment. Things were not all that he expected them to be!

There is one thing common to all the off-the-track, out-of-the-race lodgings: They are all empty. Quite empty. No one is in them, because God gave each of the owners principles to get them to run, even with feet of depression's clay.

7
Hannah—The Frustration of Appetite Denied

Dear Lord,

I would like to take a moment to thank You for whatever gift I have for writing this book. The Christian community is at present absolutely enthralled by the matter of gifts. I went through a time of great personal disturbance because some of my dearest Christian friends were delighting in gifts and bestowals foreign to the way You were dealing with me. Then a few glances in my direction denoted a hint of envy as I exercised the gifts *I* had been given. Very confusing!

Help me to appreciate the gifts You present to me, Lord, and not compare my gifts with those of my friends; for only You know what we truly need.

In the name of our Lord, Jesus Christ.

Amen.

Christian speakers come in all sizes, ages, shapes, and range of effectiveness. Everyone had told me how I would love Millie Dehnert, so I was prepared *not* to love her. I just knew she would be one of those fantastically capable women who spend the time left over from handcrafting their own luggage telling less capable women that they, too, can do anything. I was prepared for someone in stiffly starched saintliness, who had never ever had a run in her panty hose.

I wasn't prepared for Millie at all! She is cute and pretty and easy to talk to, and had just spilled a bottle of oily medicine all over her new Italian knit suit. I loved her immediately! She is also an excellent Bible teacher. The morning she spoke, she taught from 1 Samuel. Millie introduced me to Hannah, Elkanah's second wife. Hannah in her turn introduced me to the principle for dealing with the depression that comes from frustrated appetite.

> And he had two wives; the name of one Hannah, and the name of the other Peninnah: and Peninnah had children, but Hannah had no children.
>
> 1 Samuel 1:2

In Hannah's day any woman who failed to produce children was considered a useless link in the chain leading to the Messiah. Hannah had no children. Bad as that was, it was not the worst part. The worst part was that her husband's other wife did have children!

Can you imagine being one wife in a two-wife household, and the other one gets all the favors? Elkanah loved his wife Hannah. He said she was his favorite, but when the time came for him to offer temple sacrifices in honor of his wives, guess who got the smaller portion?

And her adversary also provoked her sore, for to
make her fret, because the Lord had shut up her
womb.

                                        1 Samuel 1:6

Of course she did! More than one woman cannot
function in a household without causing rivalry—and
not just in the kitchen. They can work it out, but
women are basically as competitive for their roles as
Olympic challengers are for their medals. When the
contest is over, the atmosphere can be quite cozy.
Until that time, there can be love, support, fellowship,
and selflessness, but there is still rivalry.

In the case of Peninnah, there was little love, and
certainly no support. I can just hear her: "Hannah,
I've got to run by the store and pick up the decorations
for Junior's birthday party. But of course you wouldn't
know anything about that. You don't have children."
Or, "Hannah, whose turn is it for the car pool? Oh, you
don't know, do you? You don't have children!"

Childbearing is not the only creative activity available to women, but childbearing was the one thing
Hannah wanted most. It would have given her an unquestioned place in the plan of God, an unequivocal
part in His creativity, and an unrivaled assurance of
productive purposes satisfied. Poor Hannah reacted
by becoming depressed.

Hannah was depressed because she was in a very
depressing situation. The way she dealt with her depression offers you and me a victorious way to deal
with ours.

To help us understand Hannah's victory, let's consider some of the details of her misery. Maybe we can identify with them.

> . . . therefore she wept, and did not eat. Then said Elkanah her husband to her, Hannah, why weepest thou? and why eatest thou not? and why is thy heart grieved? am I not better to thee than ten sons?
>
> 1 Samuel 1:7, 8

Every time they went to the temple, poor Hannah got a fresh set of sorrows. Weeping, she refused to eat. (Here I differ from Hannah. Under stress I weepeth little and eateth much.) Enter loving husband.

"Why, Hannah, why in the world are you so sad?"

She sniffled up at him from the depths of whatever they used as tissues. "I don't have any children, and what's-her-name has a whole kindergarten."

Now Elkanah proves himself to be pure man. "But Hannah, my love," he says, putting down his paper after first marking his place, "why should that make you sad? You've got *me*." (I can just picture the expression on Hannah's face.) "Am I not more to you than ten sons?"

Elkanah loved Hannah. She pleased him. There is nothing to indicate they were not a close and loving couple, but . . . . If anyone reading this, man or woman, is suffering the agony of a deep, repeated depression that, like Hannah's, is a result of being nonproductive, you know that one of the deepest hurts is the lack of understanding from someone very close to you.

Young couples always think they will go through everything together. But God does not deal with us collectively. He deals with us individually. Love makes it possible for us to empathize with things we can't understand, but love does not give experiential understanding. Hannah's comfort was not to come from Elkanah.

Poor old Elkanah! Imagine how depressed he would become, dwelling on the fact of Hannah's depression. One depression can easily lead to another!

Hannah did a smart thing. Instead of belittling her husband because he didn't understand her, she figured out that Elkanah was not her source of help, and went to a higher court. She went to the temple to pray out her problem.

> Now Hannah, she spake in her heart; only her lips moved, but her voice was not heard: therefore Eli thought she had been drunken. And Eli said unto her, How long wilt thou be drunken? put away thy wine from thee.
>
> 1 Samuel 1:13, 14

The highest human agent for organized religion offered her only sharp words of correction! None of that helps Hannah one bit. She didn't get understanding from her husband, and now her priest gives her a temperance lecture.

> And she vowed a vow, and said, O Lord of hosts, if thou wilt . . . give unto thine handmaid a man child, then I will give him unto the Lord all

the days of his life, and there shall no razor come upon his head.

1 Samuel 1:11

Hannah, who had exhausted the means of human counsel, was in the best shape she'd been in since the first of the chapter! With no help from Elkanah, no understanding from Eli, she applied the principle that releases the believer from the frustration of an unfulfilled appetite.

She offered her request to God Himself and asked Him to render her productive. She turned the desire of her heart over to the Lord God Almighty and promised to give back to Him that which He might give to her. That's the key! "Oh, God, if You choose to make me productive, I will give to You that which You produce through me!"

That's not as easy as it sounds. Are you praying for creativity, with plans to keep for yourself the produce? Hannah prayed a prayer not of claiming, not of bargaining, but of releasing—and she was released!

She prayed out her needs and Eli was touched by her earnestness. He blessed her and she went away smiling.

. . . So the woman went her way, and did eat, and her countenance was no more sad.

1 Samuel 1:18

I don't think she smiled because she was convinced she would have a child, but because she was convinced God would do the right thing. No good thing

will He withhold. God answered her with a son! A
mighty son from a mighty mother because of the limit-
less might of God.

She bore Samuel, the last judge—priest of Israel.
Samuel, who anointed kings. Samuel, who bridged
the gap between a nation doing what it thought was
right and one that acted under the Sovereign authority
of God Himself. Samuel, whose mother was Hannah.

Are you willing to give freely unto God that marriage or that career or that creative opportunity you are
praying for so earnestly?

> And when she had weaned him, she took him
> up with her . . . and brought him unto the
> house of the Lord . . . .
>
> 1 Samuel 1:24

Hannah did not take her vow lightly. When she had
weaned her child, her only child, she took him to the
temple and left him there! She gave back to God that
which God had given to her. It was not a casual sym-
bolic gesture. It was real. Hannah went home to a
childless house. At least it was childless on her
side—Peninnah's side was overrun with teenagers by
then.

However, you can't outgive God.

> And the Lord visited Hannah, so that she con-
> ceived, and bare three sons and two daughters.
> And the child Samuel grew before the Lord.
>
> 1 Samuel 2:21

How typical of the grace of our creative God!

Acting on the Hannah Principle

Hannah's principle has frequently pointed my stumbling feet in the right direction. I would like to tell you about one time in particular when I, too, put my appetite in the hands of the living Lord.

Acting is a bewildering profession. In many ways, it is unlike any other career. A doctor is a doctor, whether he is seeing a patient or vacationing in the Bahamas. But an actress not acting is no longer an actress. If I'm not acting, I'm not sure I'm doing anything at all!

I have loved working with the After Dinner Players, that Christian drama company I formed several years ago. Several years ago, as we began to expand our work, I was working full-time doing the directing and management plus writing the scripts. I do not act with the company, but was thoroughly enjoying the various activities that did involve me.

It was while I was watching a rehearsal that I sensed the beginning of a longing to be acting again. I knew I could not dismiss that just-beginning hunger the way you dismiss your stomach's gnawing when you've changed time zones and it hasn't. I went home and thought about it.

I wanted to act again. It had been almost a year since I had been on the stage, and I was beginning to miss it. I did not feel free to take jobs that would take me away from home for a full season, and there was no immediate opportunity for me to work in Houston. I could see no possibility for me to resume acting, and yet I had to admit I was thinking of it with real longing.

I turned the whole thing over to the Lord. "Lord, I'm going to give You this right away, before it's too much trouble for either of us. I'm beginning to want to act again. I don't want to interfere with what You want to do through me, and I thank You for the opportunities You are giving me. If You want me to act, open an opportunity. If not, please take away the appetite."

We can trust God to handle the deepest yearning of our hearts, because He has promised He will withhold no good thing from us. We can be sure that all He gives or withholds is by His good choice. The appetite we try to handle, subdue, dismiss, or deny, will nip us at the heels each step we take. It will trip us, frustrate us, trick us, defeat us, and—like the bully at the beach—kick sand in our faces.

If you have some hidden or openly admitted yearning, give it over to God. Submit it to the Sovereign authority of His will. Don't hold God to your plan! Hold your plan up to Him and say: "This is my request. This is what I want, but break my plan if You must and let Your perfect will be done."

No Good Thing Will He Withhold

It was about three weeks later that a friend of many years called me from California. Bill Roberts and I had been actors together in New York. (His death a few years ago brought loss to a great many of us and added a new dimension of joy to heaven.)

Bill was calling to warn me I might be getting a call from a film producer he had been talking to recently. The next morning Mr. Frank Jacobson called me from

California and asked me to send pictures and a résumé. I honestly thought it was a joke! I told my husband there was no way that a film company would consider an actress whose work they didn't know. There was no possible way my work could be known in California. I had never worked there!

My husband encouraged me to send the picture and résumé, so I did. In a short time, Mr. Jacobson asked me to fly out for an interview and screen test. I flew out, had the test, met the film's director, James Collier, visited with the president of World Wide Pictures, and called my husband to say the trip was a wasted effort.

We did further testing and interviews, and before I left they told me I would be considered for the role of Katje in the film *The Hiding Place*. Lorraine and I were thrilled. We praised the Lord for His wonders, and then we read the book. Katje isn't in it! Later, I was assured that Katje had been a real person and would have a significant role in the film, so I began to plan for my two weeks in Holland.

Jimmy Collier called me again. Would I come out for another day of interviews? I asked him, "Have you cast the role of Corrie yet? Could I know who it will be?"

There was a tiny, earth-preparing pause.

"You!" Jimmy said.

Me! *Me?* Me to play the part of Corrie ten Boom? How is it possible?

The night before I left home for my second interview in California, I was very aware of the significance of the opportunity being offered me. I would be playing the part of a real woman who is known and

loved by millions all over the world. I would be playing a major role in a major movie with established
stars, when I had little or no experience in film. I
would be gone from my home and my work in Houston for many weeks.

I prayed, "Oh, Lord, force me to do Your will. I
don't even want to want this if it is not of You."

Then I remembered my earlier prayer, "Oh, Lord, if
You want me to act—open an opportunity." A whole
chain of events, which the world calls coincidences,
and yet there are God's fingerprints all over each link.
God touched, used, moved, and blessed people and
incidents—and opened unto me a door of opportunity.

The wonder of that whole film experience will take
a telling all to itself. The absolute joy of working with
Julie Harris, whom I love as a special sister. The
craftsmanship of Eileen Heckart, Arthur O'Connell,
and the finest crew ever assembled! What it meant to
work for the first time with a director whose allegiance
was totally to my Lord Jesus Christ—a brilliant director, who served His Master with his craft well honed.
The encouragement of Ruth Graham's sensitive letters throughout the filming. The special fellowship
with Joan Winmill Brown, whose love and prayer preceded me into each day. The never-failing love and
confidence of Corrie ten Boom, who was with us in
Holland and most of our time in England. The special
friendship with Lillian Postell, Jimmy's secretary, and
Ellen deKroon, Corrie's companion. The dear friends
from home, Daisy and Jack Kinard, who visited me on
the set in London. The assurance that family and
friends were prayerfully involved with each day's

shooting. All the precious people whom God used to bless me with their fellowship, their prayers, and their skills.

I thank the Lord for the movie. I praise His name for every fact of that wonderful experience, but I am more grateful for the principle that it produced. The movie was for a period of time: the principle is timeless in its accuracy.

> . . . no good thing will he withhold from them that walk uprightly.
>
> Psalms 84:11

The Fulfilled Runner

One of the heaviest causes of depression and despair is the lack of creative productivity in a life that yearns for it. Much of the depression within the Christian community comes from the dearth of opportunity for creative expression honoring to the Lord.

There can be no joyful exercise of our talents unless it flows from our fellowship with Christ. The Christian artist who denies God's dictum for relationship automatically cuts off his supply of God's creative energy. That's the reason many Christians who have forsaken a lifestyle compatible with the teachings of Christ find their creative practices stale and unrewarding.

On the other hand, the Christian community, while quite properly avoiding practices not honoring to Christ, has been deaf to the cry of Christians yearning for expression in the arts. The Christian artist has been weeping tears of frustration under the goading of an appetite without opportunity.

But God never stimulates the appetite without having the meal ready! You can trust Him. God will honor the prayers like Hannah's. I believe we will see Christian drama becoming a ministry along with Christian music. I believe God has purposes other than frustration for all His children, and is working it out in His time in the best possible way.

We cannot handle the despair of unfulfilled appetites. They lodge in the stomach like stolen manna and cause all sorts of gastric disturbances. I can't cope with that. You can't, either. If you are trying to work out or work around some hidden yearning, you'll never make the course in joy. If you are trying to censor your appetites into submission, you'll never handle the curves in the track. We can only turn these appetites over to God and let Him handle them His way.

In the next chapter we'll tackle the problem of the Christian halted by guilt, but Hannah's principle is for the freeing from the mire of frustrated appetite.

Come, Hannahs of the world. God, who strings your tears into necklaces of diamonds, would have you run again!

8
David—The Burden of Guilt

Dear Lord,

It takes so much longer to write a book than I had expected it would! I thought the book would just write itself, once I got it started. It is just a bit discouraging to learn that prayer does not press the typewriter keys, but fingers do! What a discipline for me You had hidden away in the whole matter of this book.

Here I sit! My typewriter is turned on and I am not! This morning fresh ideas were bursting the seams of my just-awakened mind. Now after a day of routine activity—the ideas are gone. I can remember only little wisps of phrases that glow like tinsel fragments in the carpet, reminding me that Christmas has been here. Could it be, theoretically speaking, that I am reluctant to write about guilt? It makes me uncomfortable, and I doubt that anyone wants to read about it. Sin—now that's different! That's popular reading.

However, Lord, I know that guilt sits there like a packed but locked suitcase. You can't get to the clothes without unlocking the case, and you can't unlock the case without the key. Too many Christians are running around in rags, with their robes of righteousness locked up tight. Give me the words to give them the key, Lord, as You have given that key to me.

I pray in the name of the Lord Jesus Christ.

Amen.

During a speaking engagement at Pepperdine College, I spent several days in Malibu. One particular evening in the rosy graying of sundown, I sat at a restaurant window relishing the breathtaking view of sand and water below me. I noticed a young man and his dog jogging past, then later back again.

The large brown dog was suddenly joined by a small gray terrier, who had to jog at double time to keep the pace. The two dogs added several flourishing detours to the course, with much yelping and quick deep turnings in the sand. The human-type jogger belonging to the big dog had a much less eventful time as he kept to his course.

Somewhere out of my line of vision, someone whistled, and the gray terrier took off in immediate answer to the call. The brown dog watched for a second and then streaked after his canine companion. The young man whistled and clapped for the dog, but got no response. The two dogs were out of sight, while the jogger stood, arms akimbo, calling out to his pet.

I smiled a bit at the gleefully disobedient dog. What fun he was having! There was nothing at stake but a few delicious moments of freedom and a slightly exasperated jogging companion. I felt like congratulating the dog, who had pulled off a neat extension of freedom.

Later, I heard the sound of muffled barking. I looked out and again saw the large brown dog. He had obviously decided to return to his master, but the situation had changed. To my amazement, I saw that the tide had come in quickly, trapping the dog on what had once been a sandy runway. It had happened so quickly!

The dog tried to wade across, but the water was too deep. Now he stood mournfully barking to his master, who must have jogged on up the beach. The dog made a determined entrance into the shallowest part of the water, pressing against the water's strong current. His whole body was struggling to find a clear path.

Then I saw the dog's master come around the building. He waded into the water, scooped the still-paddling dog in his arms, and dropped him safely on the other side. The dog shook himself vigorously while his master delivered what must have been a stern lecture. Then the dog lay down meekly, head between his paws, the perfect picture of abject apology.

The master and dog turned and started off again, very much together, and jogged out of sight. The dog was so close to his master's heels I wondered why he was not kicked in the face. That was *fellowship restored!*

You may not like an analogy that brings you into the picture as a dog, but sooner or later the Christian will find himself leaving frantic footprints where sin has separated him from fellowship with his Master.

That dog was his master's dog on either side of the water, but in his act of disobedience, he had lost the joy of fellowship. I cannot tell you the number of times my own paw prints have left that dismal pattern. I could see the separating water and could feel the guilt of my disobedience, and I was miserable!

Guilt cuts across our path so quickly! It's like excess poundage. As any woman knows, all the medical authorities are wrong about weight. One month I was thin, the next month I was healthy, the next *week* I was plump, and the very next *day* I was fat!

While we were filming *The Hiding Place,* I wore a double layer of padding under my clothing to give the appearance of weight. We had been shooting in Holland for several weeks when we got to one scene in which I was to do some running up and down stairs. (I asked Corrie if she were the only one in her family who ever ran, because there were five running scenes, and I was always the runner!)

They were setting the lights before the actual filming, and the director was concerned that I might wear myself out on the rehearsals. He came to me and suggested that while we were rehearsing I take off the padding. I didn't have it on! That's when I learned that more things are wrought by Dutch pastry than this world ever dreams of!

That's the way sin happens. It starts simply, collects quickly, and settles heavily. Under its weight I felt guilty because I was guilty. I tried to deal with my guilt feelings through all sorts of procedures. I recited all the soothing excuses: "After all, it's only human nature. God understands. I just can't help it."

Strangely enough those excuses were all true, but they didn't help because truth is not necessarily excusable. But God had a plan, a principle, and a purpose for me.

When God reveals our guilt to us, He always purposes more joy in the repairing than misery in the revealing. The Holy Spirit convicts us of guilt so that we might repair the wrong, claim forgiveness, and get back to the joy of running. If God is getting to you about that matter of guilt, you can be sure He has a purpose for you that is stymied by that guilt. To help you get up and going again, here is the example of David, whose feet of clay stumbled over guilt and brought him to his knees in repentance.

David's Guilt

David was the grandest king Israel had ever known and would ever know until the true King of Kings. Shepherd, poet, general, king; he served well in all roles. Graced with opportunities and capacities few men have ever known, his reign in Israel marks the pinnacle of her history.

Yet this man, a man after God's own heart, stumbled in his running and fell under the load of guilt. Common ordinary guilt, too—not even some unique sin of purple velvet, fit only for kings.

We are told that ". . . at the time when kings go forth to battle . . . ." (2 Samuel 11:1) David didn't. The idle king rose from his couch one afternoon and, strolling around his rooftop, spied a beautiful woman taking a bath. Some things were different in David's day and some things weren't.

I'll admit I'm not used to women whose bathtubs are in public view, but then I don't know a lot of kings who go for walks on their rooftops, either. To my way of thinking, one or both of them had to go a little out of the way to get into trouble!

However, David saw Bathsheba and was affected by her sensual beauty. He inquired after her, sent for her, claimed her acquiescence as a king, and claimed her body as a man. She went home and in a reasonable length of time sent him a message that said she was pregnant. As I said, some things were different in David's day and some things weren't!

Bathsheba's husband, Uriah, had been out of town on business. He was battling the Ammonites in the skirmishes David had chosen not to attend. Trying to cover up his sin of adultery, David had Uriah brought back home for a timely visit. What a simple plan. No harm done! The child would be considered Uriah's, Uriah would go back to the business of soldiering, Bathsheba would resume her open-air bathing, David would continue his rooftop walking, and they would all live happily ever after.

Uriah, however, had not read the script, and as a loyal soldier on call for battle, spent his nights of rest and recreation on the king's doorstep instead of in Bathsheba's bed. David wined and dined Uriah, gave him presents and comradely fellowship, but still Uriah behaved with inconvenient honor.

> And Uriah said unto David, The ark, and Israel, and Judah, abide in tents; and my lord Joab, and the servants of my lord, are encamped in the open fields; shall I then go into mine house, to eat and to drink, and to lie with my wife? as thou livest, and as thy soul liveth, I will not do this thing.
>
> 2 Samuel 11:11

David sent Uriah back to the battle and arranged to have him slain in the normal process of fighting.

And when the wife of Uriah heard that Uriah
her husband was dead, she mourned for her
husband. And when the mourning was past,
David sent and fetched her to his house, and
she became his wife, and bare him a son. But
the thing that David had done displeased the
Lord.

2 Samuel 11:26, 27

The Lord then sent Nathan the prophet to face
David with the fact that the little secret was not a
secret.

Wherefore hast thou despised the command-
ment of the Lord, to do evil in his sight? . . .

2 Samuel 12:9

David acknowledged the dreadful fact that he knew
that God knew what David had done. The romanti-
cists have glamorized it, the modernists have honored
it, the humanists have accepted it, society has forgotten it—but God has despised it! David, the king of
Israel whose life had been a marching psalm to the
honor of God, had *sinned!*

Now I know that our placidly permissive society has
dismissed all the archaic rules of conduct. Everybody
sleeps with everybody else, and who cares? I am not a
moralist and have never had any appetite for reform-
ing society, but I do know that our new morality has a
few intriguing flaws.

If no one cares about promiscuity, why do the gossip

tabloids trade in it? If the old-fashioned foundations of marriage and family have been dismissed, why are we still confronted by the same old troublesome effects of extra-marital guilt? I also know that love without commitment is not love and that commitment without honor is not commitment. I am told we will soon move freely out of the shadow of the cleave only unto each other myth, but what I see is restlessness and discontent in this sexual freedom.

David stumbled over a rougher stone than customized morality. David learned that God has not adopted the house rules of the neighborhood! Why should David's sin be treated with such dazzling misery when surely everybody else was doing what David did? I am sure he sat with his face in his hands, muttering, "Why me? Everybody else gets away with it, why can't I?"

He couldn't because his sin carried the weight of his position in the plan of God. He was a representative of God Almighty to a people who looked to him for authority. Christians, pray for those who are in high places! Anytime you read of a popular figure who has accepted Christ, pray for him.

Of those who judged David in his sin, I wonder how many prayed for him in his prominence? Privilege always carries responsibility—and we are all privileged. David was confronted not only by his guilt, but by its prismatic reflections in consequence.

Nathan the prophet spelled it out for him: ". . . the sword shall never depart from thine house . . ." (2 Samuel 12:10). ". . . the child also that is born unto thee shall surely die" (2 Samuel 12:14).

Horrible! Is there any hope for David at all? Has David known his guilt and its results, only to spend eternity in their misery? No! God is not pleased to see His children wallowing in guilt! The gutter is not a suitable place for you or David or any other believer, no matter how dreadful the guilt.

9
David's Detour

Oh Lord, shepherd me along these typewritten paths.

Make me not to lie in these tempting pastures of verdant phrases.

Lead me beside the simple waters of Your truth, where souls are indeed restored.

Lead me, for Your name's sake, through the valley of shadowy truths, for there is great error in exaggeration.

Be with me—discipline my word with the rod of Your economy and support my own integrity with the staff of Your authenticity.

You have prepared a tablet before me in the presence of distraction.

Limit the overflow of my mind unto the words of Your goodness and mercy, that I might write honestly of the joy of Your fellowship.

As I speak of forsaking makeshift shelter, let me tell it like it is, or not tell it at all.

I pray in the name of the Lord, Jesus Christ.

Amen

Although my character does not have the grandeur of David's and the specifics of my guilt have not been his, I have knelt as he knelt and stood as he stood to praise the Lord for restoration.

There is a verse in Psalms 107 that reflects my own experience: "He sent his word, and healed them . . . ."

The Word of God came to me in the same way that Nathan came to David. Under that revelation, I was convicted of sin and brought out from under guilt into fellowship.

I had run away from God. I had gotten pretty far afield in philosophy and practice not honoring to His principles. I was, to say the least, out of fellowship.

I find it very difficult to forgive, and could not imagine God forgiving me! Isn't it funny how frequently we limit God to what we would or would not do? You see, God *forgives.* But in the first place, I was afraid to face God. In the second place, I thought there was nothing in the plan of God for me, even if I were reinstated. Why should I go through the agony of an open encounter with God, when there was no future for me in a fellowship I didn't think was available for me in the first place?

God used many people who, like Nathan, did not budge. They confronted me with the truth of God's precious procedure and gave me a key. *Confession!*

Confession means to agree with God that sin is sin. It means to accept God's viewpoint toward the particular sin wedged into our relationship. It means to call it by name—by its real name.

When I honestly confess my sin, Scripture says Jesus Christ faces God the Father and says, "I died for that one. Take it off her record."

However, the principle of confession does not give us a freeway into and out of sin. The truly broken and contrite heart does not plan to resume the sin for which Christ died. Sin may still offer an inviting call, but the power of that call has been broken by seeing sin as it truly is: a deliberate act against the living God.

Unconfessed sins do not threaten my eternal security—that was settled when I accepted Christ in the first place—but they clog up the works of my daily fellowship.

> But if we walk in the light, as he is in the light, we have fellowship one with another, and the blood of Jesus Christ his Son cleanseth us from all sin. If we say we have no sin, we deceive ourselves, and the truth is not in us. If we confess our sins, he is faithful and just to forgive us our sins, and to cleanse us from all unrighteousness. If we say that we have not sinned, we make him a liar, and his word is not in us. My little children, these things write I unto you, that ye sin not. And if any man sin, we have an advocate with the Father, Jesus Christ the righteous: And he is the propitiation for our sins . . . .
>
> 1 John 1:7–2:2

Notice three special points.

If we say we have not sinned, His Word is not in us. It was the Word of God that illuminated the dark closet where my sins were all jumbled together in unrecognizable blackness.

David was confronted by Nathan, I was confronted

by the Bible. It was the clinical action of the Holy Spirit that told me my problems were not guilt *feelings,* but *guilt!* There is only complacency in ignorance. God gives us peace through knowledge.

If we walk in the light, we have fellowship with one another. Being out of fellowship with God also means we are out of fellowship with one another. When I'm not right with God, I'm seldom at ease with those that are. Furthermore, when I'm not right with God, I don't even enjoy fellowship with others who are not right with Him!

If we confess our sins, He is faithful and just to forgive us our sins and cleanse us from all unrighteousness. He is faithful! He is true to His Word.

These three points make up the principle of confession. In Psalms 51 we can read how David applied this principle in his life.

> For I acknowledge my transgressions: and my sin is ever before me. Against thee, thee only, have I sinned, and done this evil in thy sight: that thou mightest be justified when thou speakest, and be clear when thou judgest.
>
> Psalms 51:3, 4

David confessed his sin eloquently and belatedly. The simplest way to deal with guilt is to handle it quickly. It's the guilt that stays there unconfessed that causes the festering.

David met the specific reality of his sin's action. "Against thee, and thee only, have I sinned." Neither circumstances, social considerations, or the honor of any wounded party change the nature of sin. It is an act against God! You may need to make restitution with other people, but the primary issue is to get right with God.

> Restore unto me the joy of thy salvation; and uphold me with thy free spirit. Then will I teach transgressors thy ways; and sinners shall be converted unto thee.
>
> Psalms 51:12, 13

"Oh, Lord," David cried, "give me again the joy of our fellowship." It is my deepest personal feeling that the great need in the Christian community today is for Christians to be restored to fellowship. Some believers are out of touch with the Lord who bought them and have no joy in their redemption. They are redeemed, because God keeps all His promises, but they are unproductive and cannot run to bring the good tidings!

David could say "I am His and He is mine, but oh, the awesome agony of that broken daily fellowship!" The joy was gone. The testimony no longer poured out from that sweet psalmist of Israel.

Out of the experience of that restoration, David would teach others. God will take that sordid detour of sin and render even that productive. Once again God is the Glorious Scavenger! Your experience of restoration is totally unique and has a ministry of its own. God will allow you to teach others. Restored, you will not be wasted! Out of that mire there will come a ministry.

That is the principle that freed David, that freed me, and that can free you. Confess your sins. Get rid of the guilt!

The elevators in my high-rise apartment building contain a lesson on confession, believe it or not! Those two elevators are not really winners.

One of them is a slow thinker. The doors open, the passengers enter, the floor buttons are pushed, and the elevator thinks about it. We prod it along with helpful hints, like pushing the "close door" button, but we never speak harshly, because then this particular elevator, which cannot take criticism, turns off all its lights.

The other elevator also has problems. It is more artistic and less dependable than the slow thinker, which will eventually get you to the proper floor. The second elevator stops on any floor that catches its imagination! Unfortunately, it becomes so tenderly involved with its playful passengers that sometimes it never opens its door to let them out. All that is needed to remedy the situation is vigorous pounding of the door on the floor where the elevator has stalled, but dogs being rushed to the first floor for their walks occasionally no longer need them!

The other day I saw the manager conferring with two servicemen. She pointed to the riskier elevator, and I felt a rush of relief—things were going to be better! When the workmen had left, I found our errant elevators still retained their personalities, but had brand-new carpets!

This is so typical of the way we try to handle guilt.

We don't repair the mechanism, we just work on its appearance. The principle of forgiveness gets the mechanism back in order. Confess! God forgives, and you can get up and get back to work—with joy.

But what about all those who have been irrevocably damaged by our guilt? The innocent ones whom our guilt splattered with mucky clay. The believer restored looks with sudden awareness at the havoc his guilt has caused. Some of it may indeed be past repair.

Israel had suffered from David's guilt. The authority he had exercised in obedience to God had crumbled in his disobedience. The guilty detours he had taken left a pattern on the trails of his sons, his family, his nation.

> . . . build thou the walls of Jerusalem.
> Psalms 51:18

"Lord, repair what my actions have damaged!" God's sovereign selection determines what scars are erased and what remain, but we can release our request to Him. God, who bends low to offer His whole person to you as you kneel in confession, will go where you have been in your error and then stand with you to lead you back into action, restored.

David's makeshift shelter—off the track, out of the running—is just as empty as Hannah's was. They learned the way to deal victoriously with the depression of frustration and guilt.

10
The Load of Despair

Dear Lord,

Please give me honest words to share Your hope with others. I am a dreamer, Lord, of some very self-gratifying visions. I can just see me standing as a benign dispenser of hopefulness, smiling as I hand out little packages of promises!

The scene changes. The swell of heavenly music blends in with the rushing of troubled waters. There I am, humbly pedestaled, heralding the harbor to those floundering in the darkness of a stormy sea.

What a ridiculous posture! You never call anyone to be a manna machine, and Your Word is the only beacon that brushes the dark waters with hope.

If there are any floundering craft tossed to and fro by my sea of words, use me any way You can. I'll gladly forsake the pedestal—my arms were getting tired, anyway. Maybe I'm just a friendly porpoise, offering little nudges toward the harbor of Your joy.

I pray in the name of our Lord, Jesus Christ.

Amen.

Of all the characters to come from the pages of the Old Testament, none fascinates me more than Elijah. The full-colored range of his emotions and the epic

93

quality of his actions carry a uniquely theatrical statement.

On top of Mount Carmel, in full view of all the people, he dared to stage a praying match with the four hundred fifty priests of Baal. One lone prophet of Jehovah God took on the masses of pagan priests and, in the name of the Lord, he won! It is an exciting story, and I encourage you to read it in detail in 1 Kings 18.

See the pagan priests screaming to their gods, dancing with increasing fervor around the altar, and finally cutting themselves with sharp knives as they threw themselves upon the altars. No answer!

See Elijah—who had a sense of timing any actor would envy—stand watching so very calmly. See him suggest to the priests that they should cry out a bit louder. Perhaps their god is asleep. Perhaps he is away on vacation.

Then see Elijah pray once, simply and wholeheartedly to his God. See the great One God answer with fire! Wonderful! See the drought-breaking rain that flooded the valley in answer to Elijah's request.

Elijah ran down from that meeting expecting a victory celebration, but was met by an order for his arrest! He was hated by King Ahab's sweet little wife, Jezebel. What a blow to Elijah. He had done his work well, the performance had been a smashing success. All the reviews had been raves. He should have been at the pinnacle of success, but instead he had to run for his life!

To put it mildly, things didn't turn out quite as he had expected. Have you been there? Have you ever known the crushing of your heart as your offering of love and craftsmanship is considered worthless? Have you sat and tried to make sense of all the hours wasted in preparation, all the sacrifices?

Before we get to Elijah's principle, let me share with you an experience of my appropriating it. I have claimed it many times, but this one time stands out in my memory with glaring clarity.

When the film *The Hiding Place* was first previewed in Houston, I experienced more uneasiness than I had known since the first day of filming. In that weird scheduling of events that makes us think the best has happened at the worst possible time, the early morning preview fell on the Saturday I was to teach the After Dinner Players' acting class.

World Wide Films graciously invited our company to attend the preview, which meant that my acting students would come from seeing me act to hearing me lecture about it! I was so uptight I thought of canceling the class.

I was uneasy because *The Hiding Place* offered, up there on that giant screen, the very best that I could do. No crumb of energy was withheld, no guarded talent was retained. I worked with full abandonment, without excuse, without apology.

If it wasn't liked, I had nothing else to offer. That was the best I could do. Realizing my students would see it and then hear me speak, I knew I had no excuse if the technique I taught had not produced the kind of work they could admire.

Well, everything turned out fine. My company was so affected by the film they could not begin to concentrate on a lecture, and we abandoned the whole program and sat together to talk and cry about the work of God in *The Hiding Place*.

That experience served to alert me to my great vulnerability concerning the film. I began to protect myself for what would surely be criticism from one source or another. When I saw the film for the first time at a preview in Dallas, I realized that I was not able to deal with critical talk about that movie. I could not be clinical about comments concerning cuts that had to be made, or length of the film, or any opinion that did not come from someone involved in the making of the film itself.

I learned to lead the conversation away from the film's essentials when I was talking to casual friends. I had to learn to handle myself without reacting violently to various expressions of dissatisfaction. My feelings were not public domain!

First one review and then another came in from highly respected professional sources. They applauded the film! My armor against criticism melted in the warmth of praise. They even singled me out for special accolades.

I began to get fan letters from all over the country. At my speaking engagements, audiences would stand in line for hours just to tell me what that film had meant to them. I heard from theater friends in New York, California, and throughout several states, saying that my work had been exceptional, and they were proud of me.

I was touched by each comment and honestly delighted in the bouquets the Lord let me enjoy on their

way to Him. I was nominated for the Golden Apple
and Golden Globe Discovery of the Year awards.

Somewhere in all that activity, a note was introduced that became a melody. Someone breathed the
phrase Academy Award as they passed by. I heard it
and laughed. How funny, that someone would even
think I could be included in the Academy Award
category. I laughed the first ten times I heard it!

Positive reviews kept coming in, and someone said
it again: "You'll get an Academy Award." I didn't
laugh or change the subject. Could it be possible? It
didn't seem so, but wonders had been done. Our film
was being called a classic in its time. It had some of
the greatest talents of the business in it, and there was
no faltering of craftsmanship.

I believed without any doubt that the directorial
work of Jimmy Collier would certainly be acclaimed
by the industry, and that Tedd Smith's music was of
such genius that it honored the craft. I could see why
Julie's work would be recognized, and Eileen's, but I
was awed by the thought that I might be considered.

A woman took me aside at a meeting to assure me
she had had a vision of my winning the award. Two
days later, another lovely lady said that she and a
small group of Christians were claiming the Oscar for
me. I was a little embarrassed, but began to imagine
the possibility.

What a joy, to carry the banner of Christians in the
theater into the very marketplace of the industry! I
tried not to think about it, but couldn't keep my mind
away from the possibility.

I was in Minneapolis when the nominations were

announced. I spoke in a meeting that morning and then spent the afternoon in my comfortable suite at the hotel. I got a little nervous waiting to hear and wished I had a direct line to the California papers. Before they picked me up for the evening meeting, I had begun to wonder why no one had called. Nothing was said at the church, nothing at the reception after the meeting, but as I walked into my hotel room, my telephone was ringing!

I snatched it from its cradle and managed a hushed hello. My husband's voice greeted me. "You're *my* Academy Award winner, no matter what *they* say."

I hadn't won a nomination. I hadn't blazed a trail in the industry. No nominations—not for anyone in the film—nothing!

I felt like a fool. How stupid of me to have even dreamed of such a thing! Very briskly I undressed and went to bed. I read a little and then, neatly tidying up the ashes of my dream, I flipped off the light and said my evening prayer. Closing my eyes, I settled back comfortably for two and one-half seconds.

Then came the tears and the pain of realizing what I had lost. All those people looking at me. The lovely ladies who had claimed it for me. The beautiful people who worked so hard with me. I had failed them!

I finally got bored with misery, as I usually do, and checked off a few facts. I *was* still alive. There would be breakfast in the morning, and when I last checked, the direct line to God had not been cut off. I had just started writing this book, and I remember saying to myself just before I dozed off, "Well, bad as it is, it's still worth a chapter!"

The next time I went to speak to a Christian group, I dreaded seeing the embarrassed disappointment in their faces. I was not sure I could deal with it. Now would come the hardest part of all: the encounter with the community I had failed.

When the club chairman came to greet me that day, she asked, "How are you this morning?"

I smiled with studied charm and simpered, "I'm fine, but I'd be a lot better if I had an Academy nomination."

Her face expressed deep concern. Perhaps she hadn't heard *the news?* Thank goodness I told her— she might have introduced me as a nominee!

I patted her hand. "I'm sorry about it."

She hugged me and said, "I'm sorry, too. What was it?"

What was it? You mean to tell me the Christian community had not been waiting with bated breath for the outcome of the nomination announcements? Could it possibly be that God did not feel those awards were essential to His plan for the arts? I couldn't keep from laughing. That lady will understand only if she reads this book. I had just learned that I had not been booked as a nominee, but as a winner in Christ!

I look forward to a time when Christian films, Christian theater, Christian television, will have an accepted and honored place in the media. That time has been brought closer by the film *The Hiding Place* and offerings of like craftsmanship. I thank God because an effect is being made by that film which will register throughout time and eternity.

I am delighted to be an actress, elbowing my way through a highly competitive profession. I would not be helped by condescending sheltering because I am a Christian. I want to learn my craft, compete with the best of them, and serve my Lord with the excellence He gives me the potential for exercising. I do not minimize the significance of recognition such as industry awards, but I lost a major one and can still run with joy because of a principle exemplified by a person. Elijah. Elijah, who was stopped by the depression of despair.

11
Elijah—We Run by Choice

Dear Lord,

I was just beginning to enjoy this when the worst thing happened. I reread what I have written about depression, and it has made me so depressed I want to quit!

I want to run ahead of each reader and say, "Look, if you don't like this I can do it over." Oh, Lord, I really thought I was well of that. Maybe I'm learning to apply a lesson that I learned on the stage. It's not how sick you are that matters, but how well you are. Even if you're sick with fear, you can still be well enough to keep on going.

Thank You, Lord, for interrupting me before I finished writing out my resignation. I'm ready to stay in the race.

I pray in the name of the Lord, Jesus Christ.

Amen.

The background of Elijah's great day on the mountaintop is given to us in 1 Kings. Israel was suffering a dearth of rain and an abundance of weak kings. The two were quite related: The weak kings had adopted pagan practices to such an extent that seven hundred pagan priests were fed with the king's kitchen budget!

. . . and Ahab did more to provoke the Lord
God of Israel to anger than all the kings of Israel
that were before him.

1 Kings 16:33

King Ahab had forsaken the commandments of the
Lord. In the midst of this is tough, God-honoring
Elijah. He delivered a message to the king from God:

. . . there shall not be dew nor rain these years,
but according to my word.

1 Kings 17:1

Elijah then went his way, to be miraculously fed by
ravens and a penniless widow. The drought got so bad
that famine befell even the king's cattle. When the
palace feels the pinch, you can imagine how badly the
people are hurting.

Elijah told the king it was time to see whose God
could deliver Israel from the famine.

Now therefore send, and gather to me all Israel
unto mount Carmel, and the prophets of Baal
four hundred and fifty . . . .

1 Kings 18:19

So Ahab scheduled a massive faith-at-work confer-
ence, to learn what kind of faith it is that works. The
people were watching with fascination as the four
hundred fifty prophets of Baal lined up against the one
prophet of the Lord God.

Elijah started the program with a statement so significant it still echoes down the mountain, across the

oceans, and over the generations, until it knocks at the doors of our own hearing.

> How long halt ye between two opinions? if the Lord be God, follow him: but if Baal, then follow him.
>
> *See* 1 Kings 18:21

What a shockingly relevant question! Halt? Yes, limping with ankles sprained by indecision, back and forth between two different opinions.

Notice he was very specific about the difference of the two opinions. It *does* matter what you believe. God said He would not be worshiped with other gods! Jehovah God is the great One God. Beside Him there is no other!

Elijah began the show, setting down the rules.

> Let them therefore give us two bullocks; and let them choose one bullock for themselves, and cut it in pieces, and lay it on wood, and put no fire under: and I will dress the other bullock, and lay it on wood, and put no fire under: And call ye on the name of your gods, and I will call on the name of the Lord: and the God that answereth by fire, let him be God . . . .
>
> 1 Kings 18:23, 24

Well, the prophets of Baal whooped it up all day with chantings, screamings, and all the nonsense that accompanies beseechings unto gods who are not there.

"But there was no voice, nor any that answered" (*see* 1 Kings 18:26).

Elijah's turn came at long last. If he had any followers, they must have felt like parents at a dance recital
when their child is last. They had to be polite and
watch all the performances, but by the time their
favorite's turn came, they were too tired to applaud.

Elijah followed the procedure of the others, but
added a little flourish of water around the wood, to
give God's team a handicap.

> . . . Elijah the prophet came near, and said,
> Lord God of Abraham, Isaac, and of Israel, let it
> be known this day that thou art God in Israel,
> and that I am thy servant, and that I have done
> all these things at thy word. Hear me, O Lord,
> hear me, that this people may know that thou
> art the Lord God, and that thou hast turned
> their heart back again. Then the fire of the Lord
> fell, and consumed the burnt sacrifice, and the
> wood, and the stones, and the dust, and licked
> up the water that was in the trench. And when
> all the people saw it, they fell on their faces: and
> they said, The Lord, he is the God; the Lord, he
> is the God.
>
> 1 Kings 18:36–39

Wowee! A five-star feature! But that's not all. Elijah
said to Ahab, ". . . Get thee up, eat and drink; for
there is a sound of abundance of rain" (1 Kings 18:41).
The certainty of faith! The sound of abundance. Everything Elijah said and did that day was right. He was
dutiful, he was daring, and he defeated the enemy

. . . and he was right! It rained!

Down the mountain he ran, a hero returning from battle. Except for the fact that no one treated him as a hero. Instead of waiting for the confetti, Elijah ran for his life. That's when he pitched his little tent of despairing depression under the juniper tree.

If you ever camp under that tree, look for Elijah's initials. You'll find mine, because I have sat there.

A few hours ago, I went to pick up my mother. After she was settled in the car, I stepped back into the house to lock the back door. As I moved through the back porch, I was suddenly touched by an unexpected wave of nostalgia.

I spent my high-school years in that house. On that porch I had played many games of Ping-Pong with teenage friends, and my mother had served countless hamburger suppers. In that green-pillowed chair by the porch door, my father had read the Bible every night. And from that same chair, he had given all my dates such a thorough interview that they must have found job applications a snap. This had been home, and from this back door I had left for my wedding.

For just a moment my throat constricted as I was touched by a second of grieving for times so very, very past. It left as abruptly as it came, but the whole afternoon carried the scent of that one fleeting teardrop of nostalgia.

That was a form of depression, a longing for times that cannot come again; times that enfolded people no longer with me. A lot of things were not what I expected them to be. I didn't know that doctors would stop making house calls, that banks would close on Saturdays, and that downtown would be filled with strangers who never knew my father.

My life has turned out so much better than I thought it would, and I am happy with things as they are, but there are times when we do not make the return to reasonable affirmatives.

I think a lot of the sadness at Christmastime is hostility because we are no longer allowed the irresponsible holidays of our childhood. A lot of times we dream up a childish expectation that reality cannot match. We find we are not appreciated, honored, or treated in any way as we had hoped.

Elijah was so tired, so hungry, so hurt, so disappointed, he scarcely had the strength to fill out his resignation. "I quit, Lord. I have had it. No more for me, thanks. I can't handle things as they really are, so I'd rather die. I didn't do any better than anyone else!" (*See* 1 Kings 19:4.)

Does that sound familiar? Three times Elijah resigned his commission and closed his eyes to die. Each time God woke him up to eat.

Elijah had a whole monologue of woes ready for his second resignation. "I've done the best I can. I've worked my heart out. I've put up with all kinds of indignities, but this is too much. Just let me die. The great work can't be done. I'm the only one You've got left, and I'm not long for this world. Even I only am left." (*See* 1 Kings 19:14.)

Elijah didn't linger there long. God dealt with him

lovingly. God knew Elijah's heart. He knew Elijah had stayed true. God knew Elijah's body. He knew Elijah was worn out. God knew the future. He knew that it was still good. And He knew a way to get Elijah into the hope for the future.

In the first place, God dealt with the matter of quitting. We don't. We tell people, "Hold on, keep going, you can't quit." God did an interesting thing with Elijah's resignation: He accepted it!

As for the hopelessness of the task, God said, "Elijah, don't ever underestimate the believing community. It's still there. I've got 7,000 in Israel who have not bowed the knee to Baal." (*See* 1 Kings 19:18.)

If you are heavy with loneliness in the ministry of your assignment, hear God speak to Elijah: "I have others." Sometimes that's a blow to our pride! Others? Could that possibly mean that God has not put His whole weight down on me? Is God implying that my personal despair will not destroy the whole plan of salvation? More often, it means the relief of discovering kinship in the assignment of God. He has others!

God accepted Elijah's resignation and honored him with a final round of active assignments. He gave him three things to do: anoint Hazael to be king of Syria, anoint Jehu to be king of Israel, and *anoint his own successor* to be the prophet in his place.

God gave Elijah three specific principles to get him back running again. Elijah resigned, and God accepted that. You can *always* quit. Remember, you run by choice. The Sovereign plan of God includes our free will. I don't understand it, but then I don't understand vitamins! God heard Elijah and loved him and let him quit with honor. Then God said, "You are not alone, Elijah. There are others."

The third principle can be the most painful of all.

God said to Elijah, "On your way out, Elijah, anoint and prepare your successor, because even if the minister quits, I don't plan to close the ministry." God completes what God begins—with or without us! (*See* Philippians 1:6.)

When I get tired and hurt and disgusted with things being the way they are, I'll probably quit, too. But please, God, don't pay attention to that. Don't give my job to somebody else. You see, if it can be done, I want to be in the doing of it. Even with my feet of clay.

12
Run at His Word

D ar Lord,

What a shock! It has b n so hard trying to find th tim to writ this book and now I hav finally cl ar d an mpty hour and th " " had fall n off my typ writ r! How can I writ anoth r chapt r in my book without th fifth l tt r of th alphab t? I can't sp ll my nam without that l tt r!

About all I can do is "in all things giv thanks." Oh d ar! I hav tri d to think up s nt nc s without that missing l tt r. B li v m , it's not asy! I don't know what it's lik in Gr k or H br w or what v r languag You us d for writing, but it's practically impossibl in nglish!

Mayb you'r r minding m that I am lik that missing l tt r. I am part of your whol alphab t! Although th " " is small and I might think it is insignificant, no oth r l tt r can tak its plac ! Thank You for that thought, Lord. Isn't that funny? About th only thing I can say without an " " is "Thank You."

Thank You, Lord.

Thank You, Lord.

Thank You, Lord!

I pray in th nam of th Lord J sus Christ.

Am n.

E

Thank You, Lord!

There *is* such a thing as failure!

I heard an inspiring speaker say once that her dictionary didn't have the word *fail* in it. Well, if you need to check the spelling, call me! My dictionary has the word, and my life has had the experience.

I have been in shows that failed, gone on diets that failed, and depended on friendships that failed. I have failed at baking a cake, putting in a zipper, playing the piano, and on and on. The person who says there are no failures is either a winner or not a contender.

One night I was speaking at a Christian coffee-house. I sat for some time and watched the entertainment that preceded me. Each engagement has its own signature, and this one's was *youth* with a capital *You!* The psychedelic lights and psychopathic amplification heightened the joy for all the teenagers present, but did no good for my middle-aged stomach and matching headache.

The lady in charge was being more energetically youthful than any of her audience. Nothing is more aging than trying to be young. Youth is an accident of time. When it becomes a planned program, it is an offense to maturity.

I know of no speaker who relates better to that mystical catchall group called young people than Corrie ten Boom. In the honesty of her eighty-plus years, she sees age as a definition, not a barrier. She is at ease in her age, so her audiences are at ease in theirs, and all those ages get together beautifully.

As I sat in an uncomfortable chair uncomfortably close to the stage, I began to get more and more apprehensive. The crowd began milling around between numbers, and the hostess was fearful that they might leave before she got me on the stage.

"Come on now! All of you! Hurry! An actress is going to talk to us now. We don't want to keep her waiting."

I wished I hadn't waited at all! If only I could move the dial of time back a few notches, to the afternoon I was invited to that coffeehouse. *That* I would like to do over!

I began my talk. My opening jokes were greeted by an impassive silence. In the midst of a Bible verse, someone's soda lodged in the machine. I think it got a hint of the program and decided not to come out!

The young boys responded eagerly. They began beating on the sides of the soda machine while the ladies serving lemonade tried to shush them. The soda responded resentfully. It shot down its little chute with such force it pushed through and past the little catch basket, landing on the floor and rolling around noisily. One lemonade lady shushed it!

I picked up where I had left off, but my heart wasn't in it. I could not make contact. Any kind of entertainer must maintain some authority over the audience. It's not a heavy-handed control, but a subtle discipline of focus. Some actors have this ability naturally. Any talent I have in this direction was startlingly dormant that evening!

I had been booked for forty-five minutes. The soda machine and I had shared but five when I left. I left the stage, the room, the building, the block, and the whole field of Christian service!

Once I was home, I tried to cry away the memory of

that agonizing few minutes on the stage. I fumed at God. "I will never, never, never speak to another group. I am not a speaker—I didn't ask to be a speaker—and I don't want to do Your will if that's what it means! Somebody else can do all those programs. I'm not going to be made a fool of!"

I felt a little better after such emphatic eloquence, took a couple of aspirin for my headache, and went to bed. The next morning I systematically canceled my speaking engagements, glancing occasionally at God to see how disturbed He was at His loss.

God was amazingly calm about the whole thing! He did not seem to realize that His roster had a critical gap. No one else paid much attention to it, either. I busied myself with several time-consuming ventures and went on about the activities of my life.

I had failed. I had planned to offer a lighthearted statement of the Lord to a responsive audience of young people. My statement had become less and less lighthearted as my audience became less and less responsive. I had failed. That was fact.

Sometimes we deal with the fear of failure. Often we deal with the fantasy of failure. In this instance I was dealing with the fact of failure.

However, I took that one incident of failure and made it conclusive. I had decided to get off the track and make camp in failure. I told God that if obedience to Him did not assure me I would never fail, I would not run in obedience to Him. Failure is inconvenient. It is also embarrassing—especially when it happens in public!

Elijah's principle didn't help me, because Elijah

had performed well. He had done a great show. Mine had been a failure. David's principle didn't help me, because I found no sin in my action and felt no guilt in my attitude. Hannah's principle didn't help me, because she had not had the opportunity I had had. She had suffered without a creative outlet—mine had blown a fuse.

The worst part of all was admitting no help from Elisha. I was not a beginner. I had tried to take what I had learned of my craft into the arena of Christian opportunity and had failed.

God did get me back into the running. Although He was functioning very well without me, He still had plans for working through me. I became increasingly uncomfortable in my withdrawal campaign. Finally I confessed my willful disobedience and came back to run again.

"Here I am, coach. Send me in."

Guess where He sent me? Back to that same coffeehouse!

"Not there, God," I said. "I've tried it there. Choose someplace else, God." I said *no* to God as reverently as I could. That's when I learned that refusing God is always irreverent. The only reverent answer to God is *yes*.

I went back to that coffeehouse with much prayer and some extra preparation. The second time around was a joyous experience! You see, there is a biblical principle that renders even failure creative in the hands of the Creator. It is found in Luke 5, where Peter, James, and John learned to run even though their feet were heavy with the crusting clay of failure.

And [Christ] saw two ships standing by the lake:
but the fishermen were gone out of them, and
were washing their nets.

Luke 5:2

They were washing their nets after a long night of
fishing. There was very little to wash out of their nets,
because they hadn't caught anything in them!

I can imagine that Peter did not enjoy the fact of his
failure. He was a successful man. He and his brothers
owned several fishing boats. He was a man of some
financial standing. He was not a novice fisherman.
He was adept at his work, but he had failed that
night.

Christ got into Peter's boat and asked to be taken a
little way out from land so He could speak to the
crowd that had ". . . pressed upon him to hear the
word of God . . ." (Luke 5:1).

What could He teach from the boat of a fisherman
who had failed to catch fish? We think success is the
only podium. I have tried to bargain with Him by saying, "Promote me, Lord, and I'll glorify You from the
pinnacle." He has replied, "Glorify Me where you
are, or you'll never glorify Me at all."

. . . when he had left speaking, he said unto
Simon, Launch out into the deep, and let down
your nets for a draught.

Luke 5:4

Can you imagine the great, weather-beaten face of
Peter, squinting up at the Christ?

> And Simon answering said unto him, Master,
> we have toiled all the night, and have taken
> nothing . . . .
>
> Luke 5:5

Peter may have muttered under his breath, "I don't
tell You anything about carpentry, so don't You tell me
about fishing! There are no fish to be caught out
there!"

I have a feeling Peter may have wondered why the
Master could make so much sense teaching the crowd
from the boat and then become so unreasonable when
He gave personal directions.

I find this type of experience often repeated in the
Lord's dealings with me. The Word is so clear when it
refers to other people. I can look at their problems in
its light and see clearly marked patterns of cause and
effect. And then it gets to me, and just does not make
sense anymore!

> And when they had this done, they inclosed a
> great multitude of fishes: and their net brake.
> And they beckoned unto their partners, which
> were in the other ship, that they should come
> and help them. And they came, and filled both
> the ships, so that they began to sink.
>
> Luke 5:6, 7

What a remarkable thing! Jesus the carpenter knew
more about fishing than Peter the fisherman. Jesus the
carpenter also knew more about performing in cof-
feehouses than Jeannette the actress. He knows more

about all of it than any of us, because He is Sovereign!

The principle that got me back to the coffeehouse and loaded Peter down with fish is just as available today as it ever was. It's tucked away in Luke 5:5. Peter said:

> . . . Master, we have toiled all the night, and have taken nothing: nevertheless at thy word I will let down the net.

It doesn't look possible, Lord. I don't see how it can work. I've tried and failed. But nevertheless, *at Your word*, I will give it a try! The principle that makes all the difference is creative obedience.

Oh Peter, listen well to His direction. He is teaching you the technique of expert fishing. He is teaching you the primary lesson of all your wonderful ministry.

Hear it above the mockery that surrounds your failure. Hear it louder than your screaming convictions about the impossible task. Hear it over and above the listing of your inadequacies. It is the Sovereignty of God, who never calls you to do something He has not already equipped you to do. Hear the truth of creative obedience—where God directs, God supplies! *At Your word*, Lord, we will let down the nets, go back to the coffeehouse—run again with your message.

13
Claim the Joy

Dear Lord,

It's such a beautiful day. From my window, I can see spring's early invitation, and I would love to spend the day outside. My typewriter knows no seasons. It always looks the same! Discipline can be so unattractive!

I thank You for assignment. I thank You for the sense of energetic purpose. I thank You because I have something to do. I trust You to give me another spring day, whose invitation I can accept.

I pray in the name of the Lord, Jesus Christ.

Amen.

Joshua was Moses' successor in leading the children of Israel into the Promised Land of Canaan. In the first chapter of Joshua, we are told how God promised Joshua that He would be with him, as He had been with Moses. God's sovereign continuity in action!

> There shall not any man be able to stand before thee all the days of thy life: as I was with Moses, so I will be with thee: I will not fail thee, nor forsake thee.
>
> Joshua 1:5

Armed with God's promise, Joshua led the people forward. The Levites carried the Ark of the Covenant—the most sacred object Israel had. This ark was so very holy unto God it could not be touched by human hands. It was on poles threaded through hoops on the corners of the ark, and carried only by priests of a certain order.

The priests carrying the ark led all the people to the Jordan River, and from that spot they could see the object of their travels—the land of Canaan. A land flowing with milk and honey, a place promised to them by God. But they were separated from their land by the river that incidentally was overflowing its banks.

Canaan is not representative of our heavenly home; rather it represents the opportunity of claiming the promises of God, His abundant life—right now. At *this* point. Claiming the joy! Reveling in the fact of all God has accomplished in us, and all He would have us enjoy in Him. It means placing our feet confidently on the sure ground of His promises. It means joy, regardless of circumstances and free of guilt. But—there is that little matter of the river Jordan.

All of the Old Testament people we have discussed so far in this book dealt with their problems and their failures by releasing themselves, problems and all, into the hands of God Almighty. Now we stand as Joshua and his followers did, with the Promised Land in view. All he had to do was cross the river and claim it.

In obeying God, Joshua had not only known the joy of obedience to God, but he had also learned of the trustworthiness of God. He probably came to the edge of the river with confidence that God Himself would provide a way to get all those people across to the other side. What did Joshua expect? A bridge? A boat?

Instead, God gave Joshua a direction. "Tell the priests to pick up the ark and walk on over." Walk on over the river Jordan? That swirling, overflowing, very wet river? I'm sure there was a pause while Joshua thought that one over!

A lot of us turn back at the river Jordan because we would rather be pampered than promoted. But some of us are deathly afraid of delight. We fear that joy may do the one thing suffering did not do—separate us from God.

That sounds preposterous, and yet I have known times when I stiff-armed the very blessed opportunities God made available to me, afraid to appropriate the Promised Land by risking the damp deepness of the river Jordan. Pick up the ark and walk on over! The Lord who could be trusted in a time of poverty can be trusted in a time of plenty!

God gives us richly all things to enjoy. This verse from First Timothy always reminds me of Dr. Dwight Pentecost—famed teacher, writer, and preacher. I had asked him to speak to a couple of our study groups, and invited him and his wife, Dorothy, to our small apartment for lunch before the first meeting. Greeting each visitor to our little home was a small handsome antique Pembroke table—a lovely piece of eighteenth-century English mahogany.

That day as I happily went to welcome the Pentecosts, I suddenly saw that Pembroke table in a different light. Every cent of its price tag was in the handmade fashioning! "Oh, horrors!" I thought. "What will Doctor Pentecost think! I have wasted money on *me* when I could have been supporting missionaries or feeding the hungry or sending young preacher boys to seminary!"

Since I couldn't burn my little table enroute, I hurried to answer the door and rush my visitors quickly through the hallway. But I wasn't quick enough. Doctor Pentecost glanced at the table as he passed. "What a fine Pembroke table!" he declared.

He recognized it! I began to stammer at him that I had just bought it—that I could take it right back and do something more altruistic with the money . . . . He dealt with my problem graciously and accurately. "Jeannette," he said, as he ran his fingers over that tabletop. "You should read 1 Timothy 6:17. 'The Lord gives us richly all things to enjoy.' The best thing to do is to thank Him and enjoy what He has allowed you to have."

God gives us richly all things to enjoy. In His season for delight, claim the delight. He can lead and protect you just as well in success as in failure. But sometimes we find security in familiar suffering, and dare not risk the unknown elements of ease. Sometimes we disobey Him at the very border of the land He promised us, because we feel that trouble has led us to God, and triumph would lead us away from Him. What kind of God do we think He is? Have we learned so little of Him that we turn to superstition instead of faith?

Joshua offered the priests the message from God,
and they lined up as directed. I've always felt special
sympathy for that first priest!

> And as they that bare the ark were come unto
> Jordan, and the feet of the priests that bare the
> ark were dipped in the brim of the water . . . .
> That the waters which came down from above
> stood and rose up upon an heap . . . and the
> people passed over . . . .
>
> Joshua 3:15, 16

The priests bearing the ark walked to the middle of
the river and stood there, on dry ground, until the
whole nation had crossed the river Jordan. Can't you
imagine those priests elbowing one another in
amazement at what God had done?

Then Joshua gave his followers one more command:

> . . . Take you hence out of the midst of Jordan,
> out of the place where the priests' feet stood
> firm, twelve stones, and ye shall carry them over
> with you, and leave them in the lodging place,
> where ye shall lodge this night.
>
> Joshua 4:3

What do those stones signify to us? The stones on
the shore mark *deliverance* by the power of God. The
stones on the riverbed mark the *appropriation* of it.

Notice that the soles of the feet of the priests rested
in the water. The water was up to their ankles before
the flesh of their feet sent a message to the mind and

heart saying God had done what He had said He would do. To know the power of God, *you have got to get your feet wet!* Step out in faith—that's the Joshua principle. Apply it to your Jordan and claim the joy of your Canaan. Then run to tell others the good news.

On the last day of my first trip to Israel, our guide led us to the Jordan River. It was as idyllic a spot as I could imagine. I saw many who chose to be baptized in these waters, hallowed by a holy history.

It was beautiful, but it did not look like the river that had perplexed Joshua. It was no special feat to cross here. "Is this where Joshua crossed?" I asked.

"No," our guide answered, "that's over there. Joshua crossed about where John baptized Jesus— over there, where Elisha crossed back from leaving Elijah."

What was that? John had baptized Jesus where Elisha crossed! One place of beginnings? The public ministry of Jesus began where Joshua led Israel to the land of Canaan!

Of course! Where else but at the Jordan do we learn the actuality of obedience? Where else do we put into practice the lessons heard in classrooms? Where else do we dare to try out our own God-granted authenticity? Where else, but at that one place of beginnings?

He who loved me so much He redeemed me would have me try the Jordans and claim His joy. Claim them in my own personhood, in the authenticity of myself.

I may cross my Jordan again and again. You may have crossings in store for you beyond your wildest imaginings. Don't miss a one! Get your feet wet! Give

God a chance to prove His power in your obedience.
Cross the Jordan with Joshua, Elisha, Hannah, David,
or Elijah—but cross it!

By the grace of God I am what I am, and His
grace was not given to me in vain. By it I la-
bored more abundantly than they all—yet not I,
but the grace of God, which is in me.

See 1 Corinthians 15:10

Dear Lord,

Thank You. Now do with this book whatever You purposed in the first place. Thank You for the joy of my part in it.

I release it unto You. Your will be done. To You be the glory!

I pray in the name of the Lord, Jesus Christ.

Amen.